Praise for The One Week Budget

Sensible, professional, sophisticated, intelligent. These are just a few words to describe Tiffany. I call her the Suzie Orman of our generation! Her daily money tips are not only helpful, but extremely educational. I learn something new everyday! I would absolutely recommend her if you are serious about getting your finances in line.

Jacqueline Nwobu
Publisher/Editor-in-Chief, Munaluchi Bridal Magazine

Tiffany was the first person who gave me real advice on how I should manage my finances. As a friend, she decided to share her opinion about why I should save. I never took this seriously until she brought it to my attention. Rarely do you meet "friends" who decide to look out for YOUR best interest. Her easy advice of saving 20% of your income made all the difference in my life. Real planning and self control has now given me the ability to buy my first house at age 27. I believe finance is equally as important as your health, and Tiffany made me realize this firsthand. I can't thank her enough...

Chris Anokute
Senior Vice President, A/R Universal Motown Records

After making financial sacrifices to start my dream non-profit, *The One Week Budget* showed me how to transform pennies into dollars by making simple fiscally conscious decisions. The Budgetnista won't tell you how to make millions, she'll show you how to save the millions you already have...and her charismatic writing style will keep you laughing all the way to the bank!

Diesa E. Seidel
Founding Director, United Initiatives for Peace

First and foremost: This book should be on EVERYONE's bookshelf! This should be the FIRST book anyone that wants to find his or her way to financial freedom reads. The budget process is mapped out in a way where everyone from the stay-at-home mom - to the young professional just starting out in corporate America - to the sophisticated investor can use. The simple steps put the system in place, and will help the reader reach their long and short-term financial goals and objectives. Soon to be on multiple Best-Seller lists and well worth the *one week*!

Chike Uzoka
Founder, Valentine Global, LLC

Visit the website:
www.thebudgetnista.biz

To anyone that has ever asked me,
"Tiffany, when is the book coming out?"
I finally have the answer.
Thank you for your love, support and suggestions.
God makes all things possible.

To my parents, Irondi and Sylvia Aliche. . .
You are the inspiration behind all that I strive for.
Thank you for setting the bar so high.

And to the Aliche Girls, "*Sistars* are doing it!"

10% of each book sold will be donated to a local charity.

INTRODUCTION

First, I want to say congratulations for trying to change your current financial situation. Even if you are here by force, the fact is that you *are* here! In any new undertaking, education is the most important aspect of attaining success. By beginning to educate yourself, you have taken the first step towards financial empowerment. It doesn't hurt that you chose me, The Budgetnista (humor me), to get you started. As you are well aware, there are thousands of books on real estate, stocks, mutual funds, entrepreneurship, and various other money-making pursuits. Like many of you, my thirst to learn more about money drove me to read many of these books. Admittedly, I read most of them for free at the bookstore. But don't follow my lead, go out and buy mine! Most of those books assume that you already have a money management system in place and let's be honest, you don't.

This is where I come into the picture. I want you to consider this book as the prerequisite to all other financial books. This book will teach you step by step, how to manage your day-to-day finances, and all in *one week*! The ability to properly manage your own money is the first step in a long journey toward making your financial dreams a reality. I wrote this book because this is the book I wish I had read when I was beginning my own financial journey. I can distinctly remember (cue dream sequence music).

I had recently graduated college, acquired my first real job and just moved out of my parent's home. Whooo hooo! It was the first time in my life that I had complete financial responsibility for myself. I was scared, really scared. Although I was not frivolous with my money (does a $5 dollar a week candy habit count?), I knew there had to be a better way to manage it. Until that point, the only knowledge I had about money was what I learned from my parents and by making my own mistakes along the way.

Despite my fear, I recognized how blessed I was: I was young, gorgeous (*unrelated*...I know) and I had no debt, *sans* a small student loan. I also grew up in a household where money management was openly discussed during family meetings (yeah). I was raised in the North East, one of the most expensive regions of the United States, yet my sisters and I lacked for nothing; (well I never *did* get that pony, but I'm so over it now). My parents emigrated here from Nigeria and were far from rich. With hard work, they were successfully able to raise, provide for, and college educate themselves and five daughters. Through all of that, they still managed to lend assistance to family and friends in their native country.

My father, an accountant by trade turned Executive Director of a New Jersey based nonprofit, has his Master's in Business Administration (MBA) in Finance. He taught my sisters and I about money on a daily basis, i.e. breaking down the cost of each toilet flush and warning us not to waste our flushes (true story)! We were held accountable for our financial choices like withdrawals made from our accounts, purchases, and any irresponsible credit card usage. My mother, on the other hand, taught me the practical side of money. From her, I learned about negotiating store discounts, buying in bulk and eliminating unnecessary spending. She was truly a master haggler. I always felt sorry for the mere mortal sales people that dare challenge her. My parents always spoke openly and honestly about the state of our family's finances, whether good or bad. Through them I learned valuable lessons about money, life and the obligation of service. They truly lived the mantra: "*To whom much is given, much is required*".

Ten years ago, I was just beginning to understand this statement; I knew that if I wanted to gain anything of value I must remember that it was not mine alone to keep (my favorite shoes excluded). I remember praying that if God would allow me to figure out the big mystery behind money, I would share that knowledge and help other people. I took classes, read books, researched and learned from those around me. I used what I learned to create a simple and systematic money management system, ***The One Week Budget.***

MY JOURNEY

Like most students and Libras, I was indecisive and undeclared during the majority of my college career. When the time came to decide on a major, I chose what I perceived to be the "safe" route. . . Business. I mean, you can work anywhere with a Business degree, right? So, I graduated with a BS in Business with a concentration in Marketing. During my last year in school, I worked in the campus childcare center. It was there that I realized how much I enjoyed teaching and hated business.

At first, I was scared to make a career change. I believed that as a teacher I would never make much money, a.k.a. I did not want to be broke. When I brought my concerns about money to my mother, she gave me some life changing advice. She said, "No matter what you chose to do, do it well and to the best of your ability. Money will follow." I have lived my life by that pearl of wisdom. With age, I have come to realize that she didn't mean I'd become a millionaire being a teacher. What she meant was that I would always make enough money to realize my dreams. It's not how much money you make, it's what you do with it. We have all heard the stories of famous people making and losing millions of dollars in a relatively short period of time (hmmm *Hammer Time* anyone?). The lesson to learn from their misfortune is this, money is attracted to those who manage it well and lost by those who do not, and that parachute pants are really not flattering on anybody! (Sorry MC).

After teaching for a few years, I began CLD Financial Life LLC. CLD is an acronym for Control, Lead and Develop. The company's objective is to teach individuals and communities how to successfully control, lead and develop their finances. CLD does so through personal financial consulting, financial fun parties, group seminars, books and my website, *www.thebudgetnista.com*. CLD also offers free financial literacy programs in underserved communities. The One Week Budget system is the foundation that my company is built upon.

The Greek philosopher Plato said, "Necessity is the mother of invention". The One Week Budget started as a system I created because I needed an organized way to manage my money. Contrary to popular belief, I am not as organized as my finances suggest. Let's just say I leave my house keys in the front door overnight, more often than I'd like to admit. My system effectively took me out of the equation! This system has allowed me to never have a car note, and save $40,000 in three years while only making $35,000 a year. It has provided a way for me to purchase my own home at age 25, with no help from "the parents". It has also allowed me to securely pay my mortgage on time during a time of unprecedented foreclosure rates and economic downturn. My One Week Budget System has also helped me in conjunction with my sisters, to be able to send my parents away on a lavish (my word, not theirs) vacation of their choice each year.

One of my favorite things to say is, "Since I moved out of my parent's home, I have never had a day of insurmountable financial hardship." I have taken on second jobs and cut luxuries when times have called for it, but I've done all this while maintaining "the fabulous". With my One Week Budget system in place, I have never worried about whether or not I was going to make it financially. I am not telling you all of this in an effort to brag or toot my own horn (toot, toot), I am simply illustrating how well this system works through the best example I know, myself. I have helped hundreds of amazing people through my company since I started sharing "The One Week Budget". In fact, this book was originally written as a few quick steps in a notebook for a friend whom I was unable to sit down with to help.

After years of sharing my system in informal financial sessions with my family, friends, coworkers, schools and organizations, I have come to this end (or beginning)...my first book! I hope that through this book I can fulfill the promise I made to God to help financially empower others. My goal is to help you achieve a clearer understanding of how to more skillfully manage your money. I know that the information in this book can do even more for you than it has for me. When it does, you can make the 'thank-you' check out to me, The Budgetnista. ☺

Enjoy,
Tiffany Aliche

Getting Started
A MUST READ
(Especially if you skipped my intro and journey)

Hate paying bills? So do I, and that's why I stopped! What if I told you that I haven't paid a bill in almost two years and my credit score is in the high 700's, low 800's? Would you call me a liar or would you want to know how I did it? With the help of *Bella the Budgetnista*, featured in this book, we will teach you what took me years to learn. It's an important financial lesson that we all need to understand. The lesson is: There is a magic about money.

What does that mean? When money is not planned for, tracked and kept record of, it literally disappears, like magic. How many times have you asked yourself, "Where did my money go?" The opposite of this is true as well. When money is well documented and used wisely, it will inexplicably multiply for the skilled handler. This is why it is imperative that you have a physical system in place, if you wish to have a financially stable life. **The One Week Budget** will show you how to successfully manage your finances, increase your credit score, lower your debt and spend less than 30 minutes a month doing so. Do I have your attention yet?

How to Read this Book

I tried to make the steps in this book as easy to implement as possible. There are 12 steps that can be completed over a seven day span. Each step contains: 1) A related antidote featuring one of my clients (names have been changed and I'll never tell) 2) directions about how to complete the step 3) an example of what the step looks like (The examples are the actual budget of a friend of mine, "Bella". I wanted you to be able to progress through my One Week Budget system alongside a real person.) 4) a condensed version of the day's Step(s) called The Easy Action Step(s) (Recap) 5) and a blank template where you can fill in your own information.

You can carry out the steps in one of two ways:

• Do them on a sheet of paper/spreadsheet as you read each step
• Wait until the end of the Day/Chapter and fill in your information in the blank template I've provided.

I've written the book as if you are doing a combination of both options. Do what suits you best.

I have also included a bonus chapter in the back of the book that speaks directly to those of you who need help with your credit and help getting and staying debt free!! To reap the full benefits of this book, I suggest that you first browse through it without taking any action. Then, choose a week on your oh-so-busy calendar where you can dedicate yourself to reading the book and working on the steps each day.

Contents

DAY ONE

Step 1
Create a List of Your Spending Habits: The Money List

There are only two mistakes one can make along the road to truth;
not going all the way, and not starting.
– Buddha

I swear to tell the truth, the whole truth,
and nothing but the truth, so help me God.
– United States Court System

Me, Myself and I
After 4 years of college, I, like most of my classmates, decided to completely ignore my degree and switch careers. My uneventful internship in a less-than-exciting work environment only cemented my decision to forgo corporate america and teach instead. It's been said that I have quite the bubbly personality, so who was I to waste it in a stiff business setting? Besides, the business world seemed too much like school, minus the fun parts and way more homework! The only downside to teaching and spending my days playing at the park with my kids (I taught pre-school) was the worry over whether I'd make enough money to live the life I wanted. It was then that I first began implementing what would one day become the **One Week Budget** system.

I was 21 years old, a recent college graduate and I just secured my first job as a pre-school teacher's aide. I was making $12 an hour, not exactly raking in the dough. Fortunately, I was still living at home (rent free), but unfortunately, I had no mode of vehicular transportation except the occasional pity ride from my sporadically accommodating older sister. So like most young grads in my position, my first official, adult financial goal was to purchase a car. Setting and accomplishing this goal taught me an uber valuable life lesson: *thou must have clear, written, and measurable financial goals*. So I wrote down my goal, chose a time frame, created a plan, used my money management system, and I saved over $10,000 that year!

Although I had not yet formalized the One Week Budget system, the steps I used to save money then, are the same steps that I use now. The first thing I did before receiving my first pay check was to make a list of all of my monthly expenses. I will refer to it as "The Money List."

My Money List (age 21):

Student Loans:	$173
Entertainment:	$100
Cell Phone:	$32
Train Fare	$105
Toiletries	$90

_____

Total	$500/month *sigh*, those were the days.

Even then, I knew that in order to accomplish my goal of buying a car, I needed a plan. I calculated that at $12 an hour, my monthly take home pay was going to be about $1,400. So if I only used $500 on expenses, this left $900 for potential savings. Do you see how easy it was getting started?

Planning my finances early insured that I didn't develop bad spending habits. After a year of following my plan, I had $10,800 in my savings account ($900 x 12 months). I know that my first major financial accomplishment may seem impossible to some. Most of your lives are more complicated and more fun than that of a new college graduate living at home. I use this early example of myself as a lesson about how a small amount of money can grow into a large sum in a relatively short period of time. But that's only *if* you have a plan.

With my father's advice, I decided to use some of the money I saved to buy a gently used, previously-owned vehicle from an auction. That's a fancy way of saying I bought a used car. I purchased the 2-year-old vehicle for $5,500 and believe it or not, I still had that car 8yrs later! Not only was I able to pay for my car in full, I was also able to obtain insurance at a super low rate. This was because I had full ownership of the car. Do you see how far into the future $12 can reach if used and managed wisely?

Create Your Own Money List
It's now your turn to create your own Money List (don't worry, it's easy!). In order to avoid having your hard-earned paycheck fall victim to designer coffee outlets and expensive clothing outlets every pay period, you must be conscious of how you spend every dime. This means no more mindless debit/credit card swiping. The little things like a bagel with cream cheese every day can chip away at your financial future. Think about your day from beginning to end. You may get a paper, buy a cup of coffee, lunch or an afternoon snack. These things may seem minuscule, but they can slowly but surely create a dent in your financial well being.

So begin by making a list of everything you spend money on and when I say everything...I mean everything! I'm watching you, so don't cheat! List the obvious things such as rent or mortgage, car note, utilities and then list the not so obvious things. Those items include cigarettes (umm, stop smoking), gum, coffee, snacks, etc. If you're anything like me, chocolate, gummy bears, and licorice will be at the top your list.

Write down everything no matter how small. I cannot stress this enough. This step is important because it will teach you to become more aware of your money. It will make you conscious of what you are spending it on. If you do not learn to respect money in smaller amounts, you will never respect or keep it in larger amounts (once again, *Hammer Time*...need I say more?). Keep this in mind during your money transformation process this week. It is easier to see how much you spend on items when it's down on paper or on your computer screen. Use the following Example Money List as a guide.

Example Money List

NAME OF EXPENSE	
MORTGAGE	DINNER
RENT	LAUNDRY
CELL PHONE	CLOTHES
CREDIT CARDS	FOOD
CAR NOTE	HAIR
CAR INSURANCE	MAKE-UP
CHARITIES	NAILS
ASSOCIATION FEES	CHILD EXPENSES
OFFERING	TOILETRIES
GAS AND ELECTRIC	HOUSEHOLD ITEMS
CABLE	BABYSITTER
PHONE	DRY CLEANERS
INTERNET	ENTERTAINMENT
LOANS	GAS (CAR)
GYM	EATING OUT
HEAT AND HOT WATER	MEDICAL EXPENSES
SEWAGE	TOLL
GARBAGE DISPOSAL	TRAVEL EXPENSES
LUNCH	INVESTMENTS
BREAKFAST	MEDICINE
POCKET MONEY	VITAMINS
THERAPIST	TRAIN PASS
DR. VISITS	BUS PASS
PARENTS	CANDY
CIGARETTES	EVERYTHING!

Step 2
Show Me the Money

The truth shall set you free.
–John 8:32 and Irondi Aliche a.k.a. 'Daddy'

Truth is by nature self-evident. As soon as you remove
the cobwebs of ignorance that surround it, it shines clear.
– Mohandas Gandhi

State of Affairs

Tony was a local politician who was canvassing the area to learn the concerns of the people in his district. During one of his many visits, he made a detour to the school where I taught. He spent the afternoon reading and playing with my students. That day, I shared with him my passion for teaching people how to manage their personal finances. To my surprise and glee, he expressed a strong interest in my services. He needed help putting his financial life in order. Tony ended up being my first *paying* customer!

The first time Tony and I met for our session; we quickly completed Step 1 and created his Money List. Although Tony did not have many expenses, it wasn't until we tackled Step 2 that I saw the problem. After we calculated the monthly dollar amount of each of his expenses, I found that he owed large amounts of money on the few expenses he did have on his list. Most of these expenses were credit cards. It was obvious to me that Tony was used to drinking champagne with beer money. He used his credit cards to make up the difference and the monthly cost was robbing him of his financial goals of investing and starting a business.

Fortunately, Tony had the funds necessary to pay off most of his bad debt in full. Shockingly, the money was earmarked for vacations rather than debt reduction (go figure). Tony was reluctant to use his vacation funds to pay off his debt. He explained that his job was a stressful one and taking vacations was necessary in order to curb the stress. It was not until we delved further into Tony's situation that we realized that most of the stress he was experiencing stemmed from several things. Among them were his poor financial situation and a hectic love life, but I couldn't help him with the latter. With my prodding, he recognized that once he had a strong financial foundation and possibly a new girlfriend, the stress would be minimized. The vacations could resume at a later time. Tony followed my advice and has stayed debt free while continuing to travel, and now classifies himself as "single and ready to mingle" (his terminology, not mine).

Tony is no different from many of us. I know you may be saying, "I would never go on vacation rather than pay off my debt". The truth is that you may have a similar financial pattern as Tony, think about it. Do you buy breakfast/lunch/dinner each day? Spend money on expensive gifts, subscribe to premium cable channels, finance luxuries (televisions, jewelry, furniture sets, etc)? Many of us refuse to reduce our spending (big or small) in the interest of our financial health, we feel like we owe it to ourselves and others to live a certain lifestyle. We do this no matter the state of our finances. I am a big proponent of fabulosity and having the things that you desire, but you must first acquire the *means* then *adequately* fund it. What changes are you willing to make to truly have what you want? You can start with a policy of full disclosure and complete Step 2.

Full Disclosure
Remember, when it comes to your money, it is always better to see things in black and white, even if it may cause a migraine. You cannot change what you do not know. The most important aspect of keeping your money is being aware of how much of it you are spending. Believe me, even Oprah keeps track, even if she pays someone else to do it for her. To begin tracking your spending, we will use The Money List you just created in Step 1 and add realistic monthly amounts next to each expense. You should start with the easiest items first...bills. I know the word alone can put a damper on anyone's spirit, but you know your bills, you know what is due. So, first list how much you pay for rent, car note or cable; any bill that is consistent. Follow up by writing the average amount of your bills that change based upon your usage; gas, electric and credit card bills.

 Tip: A quick and easy way to find the average amount of your usage bills is to take out the last 6-12 months worth of each bill (check online), add them up and divide by how many statements you have.

Conclude the bills portion by listing the amount of the bills that you do not pay every month. Be aware of the bills that are not due on a monthly basis, they need to be factored in as if they were due monthly. For example, many of you may only be responsible for paying a water bill every three months. If your water bill is $30 every cycle, then you would input $10 for your water bill on your Money List ($30 / 3 months).

Next, write in the amounts for those things you buy daily. For example, if you buy breakfast every day before work at $5 a day and there are about 23 workdays in a month (excluding weekends), you are easily throwing away $115 a month on breakfast, that's $1380 a year! Choose the cheaper option and enjoy breakfast at home or bring it with you, it will save you a few extra dollars in the end. Lastly, estimate the rest of the items on your list: groceries, clothes, grooming and candy (that last one was for me) etc. You know yourself, so be truthful. If you are not sure of the actual amounts, overestimate what you spend. As you begin implementing your budget, you will be able to add concrete numbers to these expenses.

BREAK TIME!!!! Take a deep breath, stretch, get something to drink and resume energized. You should be excited, you are about to change your financial future forever!

Welcome Back!

As I mentioned in the "How To Read This Book" section, which I'm sure you read thoroughly, the examples are the actual budget of a friend of mine, "Bella". I want you to be able to progress through my One Week Budget system alongside a real person as she works through the same steps as you. Use Bella's Step 2 example on the next page as a guideline. Also, take the time now to add your *Monthly Take Home Pay* (monthly income after taxes and deductions) to your Money List (your blank Money List template can be found at the end of Day 1).

Leave the *Monthly Spending, Beginning/New Savings,* and *Total* blank for now. We will address them later.

Bella's Step 2 example: Show Me the Money

MONTHLY TAKE HOME	$3,700.00
NAME OF EXPENSE	**WHAT YOU SPEND NOW**
RENT	$750.00
CELL PHONE	$55.00
CREDIT CARDS	$200.00
CAR NOTE	$450.00
CAR INSURANCE	$275.00
OFFERING/CHARITY	$30.00
GAS AND ELECTRIC	$100.00
CABLE	$70.00
PHONE	$30.00
INTERNET	$30.00
LOANS	$200.00
BREAKFAST	$115.00
LAUNDRY	$40.00
CLOTHES	$100.00
FOOD/GROCERIES	$400.00
GROOMING	$150.00
CHILD EXPENSES	$300.00
TOLIETRIES	$100.00
LUNCH	$115.00
ENTERTAINMENT	$100.00
GAS (CAR)	$200.00
MONTHY SPENDING	LEAVE BLANK
BEGINNING/NEW SAVINGS	LEAVE BLANK
TOTAL (spending + saving)	LEAVE BLANK

I didn't forget about you! Remember, your blank template is at the
end of Day 1. You can begin now or continue reading and fill it in later.

Step 3
Money in the Bank: Beginning Savings

If you'd be wealthy, think of saving, more than of getting.
– Benjamin Franklin

A New Patient
I could tell that Tina had been crying before I came to see her that day. This was our first session so I didn't mention the redness in her eyes as we sat down. Instead, I asked a question that I already knew the answer to. "Did you do the Steps"? Visibly upset she replied, "yes" and showed me the paper on which she completed Step 1 through Step 3. Tina was a new doctor, she was making a lot of money, but spending even more of it. Unfortunately, this is a very common habit for the YBF (young, broke and fabulous). Tina was referred to me through a mutual friend who was concerned about her spending habits. I agreed to meet with her and requested (as I do of all my clients) that she complete Step 1 through Step 3 of the One Week Budget system. Yes, I gave her homework, remember, I am a teacher first.

Tina just completed the steps moments before I arrived. She was shocked and dismayed when she realized how much money she was spending. Tina, like many of us, did not realize the full scope of her financial situation, until she put it on paper. The process of documenting her spending and comparing it to her income was both eye opening and overwhelming. After completing Step 3 (subtracting what you spend from what you make), Tina found out that she was spending almost 2 ½ times more than what she made each month! This meant that her *Beginning Savings* (the amount she was currently saving) was a negative number. She did not realize this until she completed Step 3, because she managed to stay ahead of her expenses by only focusing on the immediate bills due. Sound familiar? This system of robbing Peter to pay Paul was finally catching up to her. Many of us do not recognize that we are having trouble managing our money. It is not until we see our financial picture in physical form that we can fully appreciate our fiscal situation, good or bad. I know that there are those who avoid budgets for this very reason. Are you one of those people?

The truth can be frightening at times, but once the initial shock wears off and you put a strong financial plan into place you'll realize that there is a way out. There is always a way to rebuild your financial future and it begins with full disclosure of your current fiscal status. Look on the bright side, this step will be quick, easy, and simple....three things I love, outside of chocolate, gummy worms and naps, of course. As stated previously, being aware of your finances is imperative. This step will show you how to calculate your *Beginning Savings*. The reason I refer to this step as *Beginning Savings* is because the amount you are *currently* saving is just the beginning. Get it? In the steps that follow,

I will show you how to save more! For now, you need to know if you are saving anything, saving nothing or spending more than you make. The latter is easily achievable.

Calculate Beginning Savings
Take out your Money List and add up your *What You Spend Now* column. Write that amount next to *Monthly Spending* at the bottom of your Money List. Next, compare your *Monthly Spending* to your *Monthly Take Home Pay*. To do this, subtract the difference *(Monthly Take Home Pay - Monthly Spending)*. This resulting number reflects what you are presently saving or your *Beginning Savings*. So put that number next to *Beginning/ New Savings* (we'll get to *NEW SAVINGS* later). Low and behold, you may find that you are saving nothing or that you are spending lavishly like your last name is Hilton. At first it may hurt to see your spending habits exposed, but in order to progress, it is important to see your finances stripped down bare with reality.

This will be the first and only time I will say this...but, it is OK if you are currently saving nothing or spending like Paris. It is OK because the steps to follow will show you how to put more money in the bank and fatten your pockets!

Your last task for today is to add your *Monthly Spending* and *Beginning Savings* amounts (even if it's a negative amount, which let's be honest, it probably is). Then, write the amount at the bottom of your Money List by *Total* (savings + spending). Your *Total* should equal your *Monthly Take Home Pay*. If it does not, you've made a mistake, take your time and redo Step 3 and check your math.

Use Bella's Step 3 example to help you. Don't be too hard on yourself if you find out you are spending more than you make. As you will see, Bella wasn't exactly getting an "A" in money management either.

Bella's Step 3 example: Money in the Bank- Beginning Savings

MONTHLY TAKE HOME	$3,700.00
MONTHLY SPENDING	$3,810.00
	Subtract
BEGINNING/NEW SAVINGS AMT.	-$110.00 (Step 3)
NAME OF EXPENSE (Step 1)	**WHAT YOU SPEND NOW (Step 2)**
RENT	$750.00
CELL PHONE	$55.00
CREDIT CARDS	$200.00
CAR NOTE	$450.00
CAR INSURANCE	$275.00
OFFERING/CHARITY	$30.00
GAS AND ELECTRIC	$100.00
CABLE	$70.00
PHONE	$30.00
INTERNET	$30.00
LOANS	$200.00
BREAKFAST	$115.00
LAUNDRY	$40.00
CLOTHES	$100.00
FOOD/GROCERIES	$400.00
HAIR	$150.00
CHILD EXPENSES	$300.00
TOLIETRIES	$100.00
LUNCH	$115.00
ENTERTAINMENT	$100.00
GAS (CAR)	$200.00
MONTHY SPENDING	**$3,810.00**
BEGINNING/NEW SAVINGS	**-$110.00**
TOTAL (spending + saving)	**$3,700.00**

Day 1
Easy Action Steps (Recap)

Step 1 Create a List of your Spending Habits: Money List
Create a Money List by writing down all of your expenses

Step 2 Show me the money
Write the *monthly* cost of each expense on your Money List. Put your *Monthly Take Home Pay* on the top of your Money List.

Step 3 Money in the Bank: Beginning Savings
Calculate your *Beginning Savings* by adding up your *Monthly Spending* and subtracting it from your *Monthly Take Home Pay*. Remember your TOTAL must equal your *Monthly Take Home Pay*! Fill in the amounts for *Monthly Spending, Beginning Savings* and *Total* .

Now, it's your turn. I have provided a blank template for Steps 1-3 for your convenience.

Blank template for Steps 1, 2, 3

MONTHLY TAKE HOME	$
MONTHLY SPENDING	$
	Subtract
BEGINNING/NEW SAVINGS AMT.	$
NAME OF EXPENSE	WHAT YOU SPEND NOW
	$
	$
	$
	$
	$
	$
	$
	$
	$
	$
	$
	$
	$
	$
	$
MONTHY SPENDING	$
BEGINNING/NEW SAVINGS	$
TOTAL (spending + saving= monthly take home pay)	$

NOTES:

DAY TWO

Step 4
Separation can be a Good Thing

Nothing is particularly hard if you divide it into small jobs.
– Henry Ford (Ford Motor Company and father of modern assembly lines)

Ladies who Lunch

I was invited and excited to speak at a Women's Self Empowerment Luncheon one Saturday. The ladies in attendance had already heard speakers talk to them about physical, emotional, and spiritual health. I was there to encourage them to take care of their financial health. During the question and answer portion of my presentation, a young woman named Lauren asked a good question. She asked, "What advice can you give to those of us who feel trapped in their current spending pattern?" Lauren went on to say that she felt she had no control over her expenses. This by far is the most frequently expressed sentiment I've encountered during my tenure as a financial consultant. "There's nothing I can do!", "I have no control!", "I *have* to pay for (enter your excuse, uh I mean expense here)". These are all false statements that most of us have convinced ourselves are true. I told Lauren and the women in attendance and now I'm telling you: *We all have power over our expenses* and all of us are capable of controlling each expense at *varying* levels.

During my presentations, I normally ask a volunteer to help me illustrate some of the steps on the board. This is done to help the volunteer and the rest of the audience. After Lauren asked her question, she agreed to briefly do Step 1 through Step 4 for the group. That way, I was able to illustrate my point about levels of control on expenses. Lauren created her Money List (Step 1), wrote down the monthly amount she spent on each expense (Step 2), and calculated how much she was currently saving (Step 3). As Lauren worked on Step 4 (separating her Money List), I talked to the women about the three levels of control they potentially possessed on each item on their Money List. These levels of control are: Fixed, Adjustable, Easily Adjustable.

Low Level
Fixed expenses: expenses are the (dreaded) bills that are the same amount each month, i.e. rent, mortgage and car note.

Moderate Level
Adjustable/Usage expenses: expenses that vary depending on your usage, i.e. phone bill, gas and electric. Usually those bills that shock and awe you each month with how much service you used and their subsequent cost.

High Level
Easily Adjustable/Cash expenses: anything you can and should buy with cash, i.e. groceries, entertainment and clothes. Most of your lost-but-not-found money is probably wasted at this level.

With my assistance, Lauren separated the items on her Money List into these three categories (Step 4) in front of the class. I then asked the women for ideas on how they felt Lauren could trim *monthly* costs from each level of her expenses. Some of the suggestions posed, were to move to a less expensive apartment complex when her lease expired ($200 in possible monthly savings from low level, *fixed expenses*), avoid cell phone overage charges with a new plan ($80 in possible monthly savings from moderate level, *adjustable expenses*), and cut her grocery bill in half by eating out less and going grocery shopping with cash and a list ($300 in possible monthly savings from high level, *easily adjustable*).

Lauren's possible savings from levels of control:

Low level (Fixed expenses/Bills)	$200
Moderate level (Adjustable/Usage expenses)	$80
High level (Easily Adjustable/Cash expenses)	$300
Monthly Savings Total	$580
Yearly Savings Total!	$6960 ($580 x 12 months)

With the group's suggestions, Lauren calculated that she could possibly save almost $7000 a year. She could do this by making some simple changes and still maintain her current lifestyle! The most amazing thing about Lauren's example is that the possible savings amount is a result of only making three changes to her Money List! I estimated that if she also does things like reduce her cable, pay off revolving credit and switch insurance companies, she could potentially save over $10,000 a year! How's that for a woman that claimed she had no control over her expenses?

You may be thinking just as Lauren did that you do not have room for reduction. You have more control than you think. It's important to be willing to make the necessary changes. And of course, there is no time like the present. By separating your expenses, you will be able to fully see the level of control you do have.

Divide and Conquer
Separation, whether it be a relationship or an analysis of your finances, can both provide you with a new and valuable perspective. By separating your expenses, you can see the level of control you have on each expense. This will allow you to make the necessary changes.

Get a fresh sheet of paper. And use Bella's example below and on the next page to help you separate the items and their *What You Spend Now* amounts from your Money List. You'll separate the items into the three control level categories. How to do so will be explained as we go through each one.

The fixed category, which is the easiest to identify, will contain the expenses where the amount you pay is consistent each month. Therefore, your rent, car note and car insurance are just a few items that will fall under this category. In the adjustable column, place the expenses that are determined by your usage. For example, your gas, credit card, electric and cell phone bills will all be placed here. Finally, you have the easily adjustable column, which will house the expenses that you fully control. These expenses will typically be the ones that you can and should pay for with cash. Do not forget to add up each *What You Spend Now Column*. Place the totals at the bottom of each category. Bella was able to do this exercise in a matter of minutes. Don't let her out do you!

Bella's Step 4 example: Separation Can be a Good Thing

FIXED	
Name of expense	What you spend now
RENT	$750.00
CAR NOTE	$450.00
CAR INSURANCE	$275.00
CABLE	$70.00
INTERNET	$30.00
LOANS	$200.00
TOTAL	$1775.00

EASILY ADJUSTABLE	
Name of expense	What you spend now
OFFERING/CHARITY	$30.00
BREAKFAST	$115.00
LAUNDRY	$40.00
CLOTHES	$100.00
FOOD/GROCERIES	$400.00
HAIR	$150.00
TOILETRIES	$100.00
LUNCH	$115.00
ENTERTAINMENT	$100.00
TOTAL	$1,150.00

ADJUSTABLE	
Name of expense	What you spend now
CELL PHONE	$55.00
CREDIT CARDS	$200.00
GAS AND ELECTRIC	$100.00
PHONE	$30.00
CHILD EXPENSES	$300.00
GAS (CAR)	$200.00
TOTAL	$885.00

After looking over Bella's example fill in your own blank template, it can be found at the end of Day 2 Action Steps. Remember just fill out the 1st two columns for now.

Step 5
Reduce Your Spending

Waste not, want not
– A proverb

Expensive clothes are a waste of money
– Meryl Streep (an award-winning actress)

Getting and spending, we lay waste our powers.
– William Wordsworth (English Poet)

Keeping up Appearances
I often find myself meeting new clients in unexpected places. One such event was a fundraiser for a local charity. I was speaking with one of the organizers of the fundraiser when I was introduced to Matt. Matt was once a successful entertainer, and it showed. He was expensively dressed and had an *air* of wealth about him. We began talking and I told him how much I enjoyed helping people manage their personal finances. Imagine my surprise when Matt told me he was in desperate need of my help. A few weeks later, I met with Matt at a coffee shop, it was during that initial meeting that he explained how he came to be in his current financial situation.

Matt was once a sought after performer, but due to a prolonged and unexpected illness, he was unable to earn an income for a number of years. As a result, he had many outstanding balances and was heavily in debt. After recovering, Matt was forced to move in with his parents to begin his life anew.

Before starting his career in show business, Matt was in school pursuing a Bachelor's Degree in Engineering. After moving back home, he decided to go back to school. He used his degree and obtained a job at a major firm in IT (Information Technology). The problem was that in his new position, Matt was not making as much as his old profession, and he wasn't accustomed to a scaled down lifestyle.

During our first session, we worked through the first five steps of my system. After going through it, Matt realized that he had no choice but to drastically reduce his spending. Things like weekly haircuts (he knew how to cut his own hair) and nights out with the boys were completely cut out. Initially, he wanted to pay his parents rent, but even that was virtually impossible in his current financial situation.

On a positive note, Matt was doing very well at his new job and anticipated a promotion. I suggested that he take on an additional job and I made inquires on his behalf within my network of family, friends and acquaintances. Matt was a hard worker and I knew that in no time his income would increase dramatically. With his new financial system in place, he would be in even better financial shape than before his illness.

Like Matt, sometimes in life, we are dealt devastating blows. Those of us who adjust to our new circumstances will prosper. Those who do not, won't. Which one will you be? Do you want to start building wealth with your money? Are you fiscally challenged, i.e. broke? Then you need to cut out the excessive spending. You are going to have to resist the allure of the sales, the discounts, and items that have been deemed this season's hottest commodity. If it is not a must, and by must I mean a *necessity*, then resist the temptation to purchase impulsively. This step is easier than you think, especially when you start to see how much money you really have.

Making the Cut

Low: *Fixed*
Your separated Money List from Step 4 goes hand in hand with this step. Let's start by making changes to the fixed column. I know that reducing fixed spending may look hard since some of these numbers may appear as if they are set in stone. Being the savvy saver that I am, I have learned that there are many ways people can drastically reduce their monthly spending. Most of us are just unaware of these opportunities. And let's be honest, companies aren't exactly throwing the information out there. However, there is *always* a way you can make some changes.

One line item that can be transformed to reflect a lower number is your cable bill. Yes, I said it! Do you really need all 1000 channels? I hope you answered no. Call your cable company and say that your bill is too high and you want to know how they (keyword is *they*), can help reduce it. Tell them what channels you actually watch and ask if the under-utilized channels can be taken out of your package. No cable package is concrete; channels can easily be shaved off to save you money. Be polite, but remember that most cable companies will offer you a deal that is less than what you currently pay if you drop a few polite hints about switching to another provider (just make sure there is another provider). Often times representatives have access to coupons that they can apply to your account to reduce your monthly bill, so do not be fooled. By doing this you will be able to lower your cable bill and still maintain your normal TV routine, a win-win! There are even more ways you can reduce your fixed expenses; consider consolidating any student loans you may have, but be very careful about credit cards.

Tip: Consolidating your credit cards with one of those credit consolidation companies can be more trouble than it's worth. Although you may end up paying for only a fraction of what you really owed, you often have to pay a high upfront fee and your credit score will take a nose dive. On top of all of that, the companies you originally owed may still be able to sue you for the balance of the money. In addition, Uncle Sam can ask you to pay taxes on the portion of the debt you did not have to pay! If you truly need help with a mountain of debt, choose a reputable debt management organization instead. The National Foundation for Credit Counseling (NFCC) offers such services (nfcc.org). This nonprofit organization can connect you to a number of member agencies that are accredited by the NFCC. They can help educate you about your credit, and work with you to set up a plan. NFCC and it's member agencies can also negotiate with the credit card companies and banks to lower your interest rates, and consolidate all your payments.

Another way to reduce your expenses is by raising the deductible on your car insurance. Or, try refinancing your car payments with another agency. Shop around on the Internet and get multiple quotes. Do not stop until you are completely satisfied. There are numerous ways to reduce your spending, i.e. cutting up your credit cards. You also need to be open to making changes both big and small.

Take a look at Bella's Step 5 example on the next page. Now go back to your separated Money List from Step 4 and focus on the fixed section. Calculate the 'What You Could Spend' amount of each item and then the 'How Much You Would Save' amount of each item. You should also fill in the totals for the, 'What You Could Spend' and the, 'How Much You Would Save' columns for the fixed category. Do you see the difference?

Be realistic when reducing your spending. You can continue to enjoy all the things that money provides, but do so in moderation. Do not make any changes on paper that you will not be able to actually commit to. So be truthful.

Bella's Step 5 example: Reduce Your Spending: Fixed

Name of expense	FIXED		
	What you spend now	What you could spend	How much you would save
RENT	$750.00	$750.00	$0.00
CAR NOTE	$450.00	$450.00	$0.00
CAR INSURANCE	$275.00	$275.00	$0.00
CABLE	**$70.00**	**$50.00**	**$20.00**
INTERNET	$30.00	$30.00	$0.00
LOANS	**$200.00**	**$150.00**	**$50.00**
TOTAL	**$1,775.00**	**$1,705.00**	**$70.00**

Bold items; spending was reduced.

(Don't forget your blank template is after the Day 2 Action Steps. You can do this step now or wait and read on.)

Do you see how much money you would save? Remember, no change is too small. Be honest and make changes that are realistic. So, do you *have* more money without *making* more money yet? You should!

Moderate: *Adjustable Column*
Now let's move onto the adjustable column, also known as the usage items (i.e. turn off these lights, get off the phone, and take shorter showers column) on your template. If you find yourself stumped and unable to make changes, ask yourself, "*do I really need to spend this much on this item*" or "*do I really need this expense in order to live day to day?*" Most times I am sure the answer to both questions would be no!

There are so many ways to cut costs. Something as simple as switching regular light bulbs to energy saving bulbs can reduce your electric bill. You can also call your credit card company and ask them to lower your rate. If you have been a good customer for some years or have good credit, your company should comply. However, if they give you trouble, which some of them will, let them know that you will gladly take your business somewhere else. You can always try and transfer your balance to a credit card with a lower interest rate. Do not be afraid to bargain. Remember, persistence and politeness is key to getting what you want. So, pick up the phone and negotiate until you are satisfied and able to squeeze some savings out of this column. Bella did.

Bella's Step 5 example: Reduce Your Spending: Adjustable

Name of expense	ADJUSTABLE		
	What you spend now	What you could spend	How much you would save
CELL PHONE	**$55.00**	**$45.00**	**$10.00**
CREDIT CARDS	**$200.00**	**$175.00**	**$25.00**
GAS AND ELECTRIC	**$100.00**	**$90.00**	**$10.00**
PHONE	$30.00	$30.00	$0.00
CHILD EXPENSES	$300.00	$300.00	$0.00
GAS (CAR)	**$200.00**	**$175.00**	**$25.00**
TOTAL	**$885.00**	**$815.00**	**$70.00**

Bold items; spending was reduced.

Just out of curiosity, did you save any more money? I'm sure it is much more than you anticipated. Don't you love the idea of having more money without making more? If you stick to the changes you have committed to on paper, this idea can become a reality.

High: *Easily Adjustable*
I saved the best for last. Now let's address the items in your easily adjustable column or your cash items. This is where the most progress will be made. Since this is the column that you have the most control over, it will be easier for you to decide what changes you can make to cut down on your spending.

If you are buying breakfast, lunch, and dinner *every* day, you are flushing money down the toilet literally. That money could potentially be a contribution to your future savings. Now, I am not saying *never* buy breakfast or lunch, because I like a bagel with cream cheese every now and then too. But would it hurt you to bring food from home? Probably not. I guarantee that with a little menu planning, your eating out costs will be reduce drastically and you may even lose a little weight in the process!

Since the easily adjustable column holds the items you should buy with cash, you should be able to make the most changes here. Keep in mind that when it comes to your money, no change is too small. Something as little as getting a smaller coffee each morning can add up down the line. I cannot stress this enough; remember not to make changes on paper that you cannot commit to in real life. Everything that I am telling you is based on my own personal experiences and those that I have helped. I went through these same exercises and changes in my life (still do) and the result was well worth it. Bella was able to savemore than double the amount of money here than the other two sections combined; so stick to the changes you have committed to on paper and you will see dramatic results. Oh, and don't forget to add up the totals for these two columns.

Bella's Step 5 example: Red uce Your Spending: Easily Adjustable

Name of expense	EASILY ADJUSTABLE		
	What you spend now	What you could spend	How much you would save
OFFERING/CHARITY	$30.00	$30.00	$0.00
BREAKFAST	**$115.00**	**$50.00**	**$65.00**
LAUNDRY	**$40.00**	**$30.00**	**$10.00**
CLOTHES	**$100.00**	**$50.00**	**$50.00**
FOOD/GROCERIES	**$400.00**	**$375.00**	**$25.00**
HAIR	**$150.00**	**$100.00**	**$50.00**
TOILETRIES	**$100.00**	**$85.00**	**$15.00**
LUNCH	**$115.00**	**$50.00**	**$65.00**
ENTERTAINMENT	**$100.00**	**$75.00**	**$25.00**
TOTAL	**$1,150.00**	**$845.00**	**$305.00**

Bold items; spending was reduced.
Use blank template after Day 2 Easy Action Steps

Day 2
Easy Action Steps (Recap)

Step 4 Separation can be a Good Thing

Separate your Money List into three levels of control; (low) Fixed, (moderate) Adjustable, (high) Easily Adjustable.

Step 5 Reduce your Spending

Reduce your spending in each level, and add up the totals of the changes made. Roll around in all the extra cash you will now be saving (optional). Use the **Tips for Realistically Reducing your Spending** located in the Appendix to help.

 Sidenote: I have provided a blank template for Steps 4 and 5 for your convenience.

Blank template for Step 4 & 5

FIXED			
Name of expense	What you spend now	What you could spend	How much you would save
	$	$	$
	$	$	$
	$	$	$
	$	$	$
	$	$	$
	$	$	$
TOTAL	$	$	$
ADJUSTABLE			
Name of expense	What you spend now	What you could spend	How much you would save
	$	$	$
	$	$	$
	$	$	$
	$	$	$
	$	$	$
	$	$	$
TOTAL	$	$	$
EASILY ADJUSTABLE			
Name of expense	What you spend now	What you could spend	How much you would save
	$	$	$
	$	$	$
	$	$	$
	$	$	$
	$	$	$
	$	$	$
TOTAL	$	$	$

Is there a little more change in your pockets? I am sure there is. Continue on to Step 6 to see how much money you were wasting. I promise you that it will take less than 2 minutes.

Reminder: For more tips on how to cut back on your spending, check out *Tips for Realistically Reducing your Spending* in the Appendix.

NOTES:

DAY THREE

Step 6
Have More Money: New Savings

More, More, More. How do ya like it? How do ya like it?
– The Andrea True Connection (70's disco band)

Moving Out
At age 22, I started a new teaching job and met two new, young teachers named Renee and Monique. We all began working at the same time as new teachers, and earned the same income that year, $39,000 ($2,000 monthly take home pay). We had a lot in common; each of us lived at home, enjoyed hanging out with our friends and liked shopping. Despite our similarities, there was one glaring difference; Monique and I were saving money each month while Renee was not saving at all.

When Monique, Renee and I first met, we talked about how much we wanted to move out on our own. By that time, I had just purchased my first car. I decided to use the same principals to save for an apartment that I used to buy the car. Monique noticed how proficient I was at managing my finances and asked for my help. Although the three of us had the same goal, Monique and I set up a financial plan to accomplish our goal by the end of the year, but Renee did not.

To start, I had Monique complete a version of Step 1 through Step 3 so that she could calculate what she was currently saving. The amount was about $400 a month. That was not enough for Monique to move out. She needed to save enough for the cost of rent, utilities, groceries and other monthly expenses. I told her that she should also include the amount she wanted to save each month after moving out.

Like Monique, this is the question you should ask yourself before committing to a financial change that requires scheduled monthly payments: Am I currently saving more than what the new additional payments will cost me each *month*?

List of *new* monthly expenses (monthly expenses Monique will have to pay while living in an apartment with a roommate):

Rent	$500
Utilities	$50
Cable/Phone/Internet	$50
Groceries/Toiletries	$150
Desired savings	$400
Total	$1,150

Note: If Monique was paying the same amount of rent ($500) to her parents (before moving out), she would not have to include rent on her list of *new* expenses.

After doing the steps, Monique realized that she would have to adjust her spending to save at least $1,150 in order to accomplish her goal. This amount includes the $400 she was already saving each month. She separated her Money List (Step 4) and began to reduce her spending (Step 5). After reducing her spending and calculating her *New Savings* amount (Step 6), Monique estimated she could save an additional $800 a month. If she added the $800 to the $400 she was already saving, that was a total of $1,200. That would be $50 more than what she needed to save!

Monique stuck to her budget and in five months she had $6,000 ($1200 x 5)! She was able to move out, purchase (not finance) furniture and still had money left in her savings account. Ironically, after moving out, Monique was now saving $450; the $400 she set aside as desired savings on her list of new expenses, and the extra $50 she found after completing Step 6. This was $50 more than when she lived at home! If she continues to analyze her finances before making any financial decisions, her savings will continue to grow. Monique is a great example of how important it is to see how much money you could potentially save before making financial changes.

 Sidenote: What happened to Renee? She *still* lives at home. I suspect one day I'll get a phone call requesting help to get her finances organized.

More Money
What will your *New Savings* amount be? To find out, go back to your list from Step 5. Take the *fixed, adjustable* and *easily adjustable* totals from the "How much you would save" column and add them up. Now take the number you had from Step 3 (which reflects your *Beginning Savings)* and add it to the totals from Step 5 (the "How much you would save" amounts*)*. This is your *New Savings* amount.

Bella was able to save over $300 dollars! Can you beat her *New Savings* amount?

Bella's Step 6 example: Have More Money: New Savings

FIXED	
NAME OF EXPENSE	How much you would save
RENT	$0.00
CAR NOTE	$0.00
CAR INSURANCE	$0.00
CABLE	$20.00
INTERNET	$0.00
LOANS	$50.00
TOTAL	$70.00

ADJUSTABLE	
NAME OF EXPENSE	How much you would save
CELL PHONE	$10.00
CREDIT CARDS	$25.00
GAS AND ELECTRIC	$10.00
PHONE	$0.00
CHILD EXPENSES	$0.00
GAS (CAR)	$25.00
TOTAL	$70.00

Bella's 'how much you would save' Column Totals

FIXED (see previous grids)	TOTAL	$70.00
ADJUSTABLE (see previous grids)	TOTAL	$70.00
EASILY ADJUSTABLE (see previous grids)	TOTAL	$305.00
		add
How much you would save	TOTAL	$445.00
BEGINNING SAVINGS (STEP 2)		$-110.00
		add
NEW SAVINGS AMOUNT		$335.00

I've provided a blank template for you to find your *New Savings* amount.
See how considerate I am?

Your 'how much you would save' Column Totals

FIXED (see your grid from Step 5)	TOTAL	$
ADJUSTABLE (see your grid from Step 5)	TOTAL	$
EASILY ADJUSTABLE (see your grid from Step 5)	TOTAL	$
		add
How much you would save	TOTAL	$
BEGINNING SAVINGS (STEP 2)		$
		add
NEW SAVINGS AMOUNT		$

The number you just calculated reflects your *New Savings* amount. I told you that
you could have more money without making more. See what making a few changes
can do? Now if you are still not saving enough or nothing at all then, "Houston...
we have a problem". You will have to go back to Step 5 (reduce your spending) and
make bigger changes. You may have to cut out your cable all together, get a second
job, or even darel say it, move back home! I did it (I'll explain later in the bonus chapter;
Debt and Credit, My Story). If you are spending more money than you make, big changes
are needed in your life. Organize your finances. Make your financial well being a priority
and stop spending on nonessential items. According to Webster's Dictionary, essential
means: absolutely necessary; indispensable; vital. What definition are *you* using? Is your
definition keeping you in financial bondage?

 **For more tips about making bigger changes, check out the *Big Changes* section in
the Appendix.**

Step 7
Revamp Your Money List

If you've lost focus, just sit down and be still.
Take the idea and rock it to and fro.
Keep some of it and throw some away and it will renew itself.
You need do no more.
– Clarissa Pinkola Estes (poet)

More Money, More Savings

My college friend, Lisa, contacted me about a year ago. She told me that she was moving back to New Jersey because of her new job, Lisa was hired as a Human Resources executive at a well known fashion label. Along with the exciting new environment, the position paid more than what she was currently making. I reminded Lisa that it was important for her to update her budget, she could do this by revamping her Money List to reflect her new income.

It is disturbingly common for people to make more money, but not save more. You must plan in advance if you want to maximize an increase in pay. One of the ways Lisa wanted to maximze her raise was by purchasing rental property. Her finances were in fair order, she was now making $100,000 a year, 10% ($10,000) of which she invested in her company's 401k retirement plan. She had just finished paying off her student loans and had $5000 in credit card debt which she planned to pay off with the bonus from her new job.

Lisa was saving about $500 a month in cash. The problem was, Lisa felt that she should be saving more and I agreed. We reviewed her old budget, reduced her spending (Step 5), factored in her increase, calculated her *New Savings* (Step 6), and revamped her Money List (Step 7). These changes resulted in Lisa finding an additional $500 in savings! She could now save a total of $1,000 a month in cash. Lisa anticipates going back to school for her Master's in Business Administration (MBA); her company would pay for it, and after completing her Masters, she would be able to earn even more. If she continues to decrease her debt and earn more, she would soon have enough to afford rental property; this would in turn increase her income, savings and investments. Remember, while completing Step 7, that this step should be revisited whenever you make any changes to your finances. It is important that you revamp your Money List to reflect any changes in your financial life.

Make the Change

Now that your spending has been reduced, your Money List needs to be revamped. Go back to it and incorporate the new numbers from Step 5 (your *how much you could spend* amounts) and Step 6 (your *New Savings*). Also add up your new *Monthly Spending*.

Now pat yourself on the back, your monthly spending has been reduced, your savings has increased and your budget has been balanced. (Remember that your *Total* from Step 7 must still equal your *Monthly Take Home Pay)*. If it does not, you made a mistake, so go back and redo your math! Once again, use Bella's revamped list on the next page to help you. Do you see how she substituted new amounts to reflect her new spending habits?

Bella's Step 7: Revamp Your Money List

MONTHLY TAKE HOME		$3,700.00
MONTHLY SPENDING		$3,365.00
		subtract
BEGINNING/NEW SAVINGS AMT.		$335.00

NAME OF EXPENSE		What you could spend
CAR NOTE		$450.00
CAR INSURANCE		$275.00
OFFERING/CHARITY		$30.00
GAS AND ELECTRIC		$90.00
CABLE		$50.00
PHONE		$30.00
INTERNET		$30.00
LOANS		$150.00
BREAKFAST		$50.00
LAUNDRY		$30.00
CLOTHES		$50.00
FOOD/GROCERIES		$375.00
GROOMING		$100.00
CHILD EXPENSES		$300.00
TOILETRIES		$85.00
LUNCH		$50.00
ENTERTAINMENT		$75.00
GAS (CAR)		$175.00
MONTHY SPENDING		$3,365.00
BEGINNING/NEW SAVINGS		$335.00
TOTAL (spending + saving)		$3,700.00

Ok, if you need to take a break, now is the time. Come back refreshed and re-focused. Step 8 is very important, so read (and only read) it carefully and more than once if necessary.

Step 8
Define your Dollars I

I do my best to avoid difficulties and any kind of complications.
I like everything around me to be clear as crystal and completely calm.
– Alfred Hitchcock (Filmmaker/Producer)

I believe the ability to think is blessed.
If you can think about a situation, you can deal with it.
The big struggle is to keep your head clear enough to think.
– Richard Pryor(Stand-up Comedian, Actor, Writer)

Jackpot!
Keri was one of my closest friends. One day she called to tell me that she came into a large sum of money. A five-year-old lawsuit was finally settled and she was being awarded $50,000. After pondering upon and deciding against the wisdom of asking for a loan/gift, I told Keri that she should begin defining her dollars *before* receiving her money.

Each dollar that you acquire should have a clear purpose. It does not matter whether it is a cash settlement or your normal monthly take home pay. Each of your dollars should be allocated to one of the following accounts: *Deposit, Bills, Emergency Savings, Long Term Savings* or C*ash* (explained further in Step 8).

I suggested that Keri deposit her settlement award into a high yield money market account (it's like a savings account that pays more interest) until she was sure how she wanted to allot her new found mini-fortune. She followed my advice and with the help of her accountant, Carmen, she allocated her funds in the most profitable way possible.

Keri's Allocation:

$12,000	to pay off car note
$18,000	to pay off credit cards
$10,500	to partially pay off student loans
$9,000	savings and future investments
$500	to splurge a.k.a SHOPPING SPREE!!!
_____	
$50,000	total money from lawsuit

Keri did not have the best credit, so her accountant suggested that instead of paying off all of her debt in one lump sum, she should continue to make monthly payments. I know you might be scratching your head and thinking, what?! Your next question might be, "If Keri has the money, wouldn't it be smarter to pay everything off now and avoid unnecessary interest fees?" See, you're getting more financially savvy already. Well, you are right and wrong. One of the "things" the credit bureau uses to calculate your credit score is a consistent and on time payment history. Carmen had Keri transfer the balances of her credit cards and car note to accounts with zero and low interest rates. She then had Keri deposit her money into a money market account that yielded a higher interest rate than the combined average rate of the debt she owed. Keri also transferred her car loan to her credit union. By doing this, she was able to get a much better rate by putting down $5000 of the $12000 lump sum she set aside for the car.

She then divided the rest of the money, which was $7,000, into twelve months. That way, she could pay off the rest of the car loan in a year (this included interest). Keri also transferred all her credit card debt to a card that advertised 0% interest for the *first six months*. She made sure to divide the $18,000 she set aside for revolving credit into *six* payments so that she would never have to pay interest on the balance on the new card. Her student loan did not need to be touched because the interest rate was already very low. Still confused? Ok, let me take it to the board for the class (yes, another teacher reference).

Old interest rates of Keri's accounts:

Car note	7.6%
Credit Cards	13% (average rate of all cards)
Student Loan	3.9%
Total	24.5%
Total average rate	8.17%

Keri was paying an average of 8.17% (24.5% / 3) in interest and was making no money on the money she used to pay her bills.

New interest rates of Keri's accounts:

Car note	6.5% (with credit union)
Credit Cards	0% (average rate of all cards)
Student Loan	3.9%
Total	10.4%
Total average rate	3.47%

Keri is now paying an average of 3.47% in interest (10.4% / 3). She placed her lawsuit money into an account that yielded her 4% (depending on when you read this book that rate may seem really low or really high). Her money is earning her .53% (4%-3.4%)!!

I know it's not exactly break out the bubbly money, but it's more than what most savings accounts at banks are giving out these days. Now, not only is Keri making money off interest and reducing her debt, she is also simultaneously increasing her credit score! Now all of her settlement money (minus the $500 splurge money) is working for her. She made this happen by decreasing debt, reducing her interest rates and increasing her credit rating, a win-win-win!

Are your dollars defined? This is an important step on the road to a strong financial foundation. This crucial step is one of the most critical parts of this system. *Read* this step thoroughly today so that you will be prepared to implement it tomorrow.

NOTES:

Step 8
Define your Dollars II
(Day 3: Read only / Day 4: Implement)

Having a purpose is the difference between making a living and making a life.
- Tom Thiss (motivational speaker)

Efforts and courage are not enough without purpose and direction.
- John F. Kennedy (the 35th President of the United States)

Every Penny has its Place
Each dollar you earn should have a meaningful purpose. This step will help you define the roles that each of your dollars play in the grand scheme of your finances. This step will also help you understand the importance of segmenting your money. There are five accounts that you should set up: *Deposit Account, Bills Account, Emergency Account, Long Term Savings Account* and good old fashioned *Cash*. This may seem like a lot to do, but I assure you it's a lot easier than dodging creditors on the phone. Don't worry. It will be simple and painless and you will get a better understanding of why I stress the importance of compartmentalizing your money.

Keep in mind that before you open any new accounts, you should have a retirement account (401k, IRA, 403b, or SEP if self employed) where you strive to contribute a minimum of 10% of your gross income (how much you make before taxes and deductions). Ask your employer, financial advisor or your local bank about your options.

Deposit Account
This account should be a checking account, and it will be the primary "mover and shaker" of your finances. It should be the account your debit card is linked to and where your cash would wait until you withdraw it. It is also where all your hard-earned money would land before you transfer it to other accounts. If you don't already have a checking account, I highly suggest you go to your nearest bank and open one! Most banks offer free checking accounts. If your bank does not, then you should choose a bank that does. The goal is to keep as much of your money as possible, so do not lose your money to unnecessary bank fees. As you progress through the system, you should automate your transfers to your other accounts (*Bills, Emergency Savings and Long Term Savings*) from this account.

If your job offers direct deposit, sign up for it as soon as possible or when you open up your new checking account. By choosing the direct deposit option when receiving your paycheck, not only will you ease some of the tension of managing your finances but you will also become a little *greener* and more eco-friendly in the process. Other benefits to direct deposit is that many jobs' direct deposits arrive a day before the paper checks, so you are paid sooner rather than later. Also, many banks offer additional incentives to customers with direct deposit.

Bills Account
This account will be solely for bills and should be a free checking account as well. It is extremely important because your monthly bills will be drawn from this account. Having a Bills account will keep you from over-drafting or 'accidentally' spending your bill money. Another thing you may want to look into is online banking. With this service, you can check your balance online, receive notifications of changes in your account, and set up automatic bill payments. It will help you make eco-friendly bill payments on time and without the hassle of stamps and checks.

Online Banking
By having your bills *automatically* withdrawn from your account, you will no longer have to worry about locating paper bills or struggling to get checks posted to your creditors on time. The bank does it for you! However, you do need to ensure that you have the funds available for any pending bill payments. If you are not comfortable with companies having access to your accounts, you can also pay the bills yourself through online bill pay.Setting up is easy, painless and it should be free. Look for the bill pay option on your bank's website and follow the instructions. Make sure you have all the account numbers, addresses and due dates to the bills you currently pay, and in no time, you will be finished. The cool thing about online bill pay is that virtually anything can be paid through this option. I even pay my charity, tithes and offerings this way. As long as there is an address, the bank will cut the check and mail out the payment for you. Banks have made our lives easier this way. You can now pay your bills quickly, efficiently and postage free! Some companies, like my car insurance company, offer discounts to customers who pay this way. The goal is to keep as much of your money as possible, and by setting up an online banking account and automatic bill pay.

I promised that I would show you how to get like me! Welcome to my world of easy, breezy, financial management. With your new automated system in place you no longer have to pay your own bills! Now your only job is to check bi-weekly that they *were* paid and the checking shouldn't take more than 15 minutes each time.

Savings
By now you should know how much money you can save each month (*New Savings*, Step 6). Take the time now to decide how much of your *New Savings* you want to allocate to your Emergency Account and how much towards your Long Term Savings Account each month.

Emergency Account

Keep your minor emergency fund in this checking account. Now when I say emergencies, I mean real emergencies like car problems, unforeseen medical expenses, unexpected childcare expenses, etc. I'm not talking about emergencies like tickets to the championship game or the newest Louis Vuitton. Keep that in mind when you dip into this account, because it is imperative that you return the money. Decide now how much emergency money you want to keep in this account. Is it $200, $500, $1000? The choice is yours. Just remember that if you dip below your designated amount, you must replenish it so that you are prepared for any unanticipated minor *emergencies*.

Long Term Savings Account

This account should be a savings or money market account.

 Note: I prefer a money market account for long term saving. A MMA is usually thought of as a longer-term, less liquid investment. Banks give higher than average interest rates in comparison to savings accounts.

Your Long Term Savings Account is where you will keep money for big purchases, future investments, and major emergencies. Keep in mind that you should have at least three to twenty-four months worth of major emergency money set aside in case you become unemployed. The number of months you need depends on how quickly you believe you can find a job if let go from your current job.

We all dream about living the luxurious life, but if you do not plan accordingly or set aside money, that dream will just be a dream deferred. The most important thing about this account is the amount of interest you will receive. Interest is the money a bank gives you for keeping your money with them, so the higher the interest rate, the more cash you earn on your money. Who wouldn't want a bank to give them money the legal way? I know I would! So just keep an eye on the interest rates that banks are offering when searching for your Long Term Savings Account.

One website that I recommend when perusing for banks is www.bankrate.com. Bankrate. com provides free rate information to consumers on more than 300 financial products. Those products include mortgages, credit cards, new and used automobile loans, money market accounts, CDs, checking and ATM fees, home equity loans and online banking fees. It is a very useful site. I use it every time I look for a new money market account. As you use Bankrate or any other financial information site, it is important to know what to look for. I have provided a detailed list to help you choose wisely, you can thank me later.

Bank Criteria

- The most essential quality in a bank is that it is FDIC insured. This means that the federal government insures that your money in the bank is protected up to a certain amount. The amount could be anywhere from $100,000- $250,000 per depositor, per insured bank.
- Choose the highest APY* (Annual Percentage Yield). In laymen's terms... the yearly interest the account yields.
- The amount needed to open up an account should be low.
- Avoid fees! The amount of fees you have to pay should equal $0. You do not want to pay the bank money if your account dips below a certain amount. Remember, the goal is to keep as much of your money as possible.
- Your interest should compound daily. You want your money to work hard for you every day. You work hard for it, so it should work for you!
- The bank should be a sound and safe place to keep your money. Bankrate has a star system that rates banks soundness (safeness). The more stars, the safer the bank.

 Quick Tip: Link your Deposit Account to your Long Term Savings Account so you can transfer your money for savings automatically.

While visiting websites like Bankrate.com, explore them, learn them, and love them! Click on anything that you are unsure of and read about it. Websites like these will help broaden your financial knowledge, and help you pick the best bank for your buck. Read on and take in all new financial information. See, you're already becoming a financial connoisseur and it is only Day 3!

The Cash Account
Let me clarify something first, this is not an actual account. It is just cold, hard cash. Think of your cash as your biweekly allowance (whoever thought you'd be getting allowance at your age)! It may be in your best interest to divide your biweekly cash in half and give yourself a weekly allowance. It will sit in your Deposit Account until it needs to be withdrawn. The reason I listed this as a separate account is to get you in the habit of mentally compartmentalizing your money.

It is almost always best to pay cash versus a credit card, debit card or check. This is because it cuts down on credit card debt, overdraft mistakes, and keeps you more aware of how much you are actually spending. There is evidence that shows consumers spend 18% more on average when using a credit card vs. cash (JW PerkStreet Financial). When you use your debit card or credit card to purchase something, oftentimes the money does not feel real, so you end up spending more. When you pay with cash you actually see and feel your money leaving your grasp. It is a painful thing sometimes, because with cash, you know your money is going to someone else, therefore prompting you to spend less.

Note: I suggest that you *do not* **pay cash when you donate money to a religious organization or charity. Write a check or use online bill pay and let the bank write the check for you. You will need proof of your donations for your tax records. These types of contributions are tax deductible thereby keeping more money in your pocket.**

Armed with Cash

Leave your credit cards at home and resist the temptation of financing. You will save money this way and reduce unnecessary spending. How many of you have financed big purchases and now you have a bedroom set bill, a couch bill and a T.V. bill? These bills are snatching your potential savings out of the bank before they get there! They are not essential, and they are causing detrimental harm to your finances. I am here to be the voice of reason, and say...STOP! You will not die if you do not have that brand new flat screen T.V. If you truly want it, save up the money and buy it with cash instead of financing it.

When you are armed with cash, you have the upper hand. Many times, you can use it to bargain your way to a more attractive price of your liking. Thanks to my mother, the master bargain negotiator, I learned how, and do it all the time. Financing just adds more money onto the original price. The interest rate drives the cost up and you will end up dishing out more money than the actual cost of the item. Let's face it, it's probably overpriced to begin with.

Day 3
Easy Action Steps (Recap)

Step 6   Have More Money: *New Savings*
Calculate your *New Savings* by adding the '*How much you would save*' totals and your *Beginning Savings* from Step 3.

Step 7   Revamp Your Money List
Go back to your Money List and add the *What You Could Spend* amounts, your new *Monthly Spending, New Savings* and *Total.*

Step 8   Define Your Dollars (read only)
Read this step and plan a day to implement it.

Tomorrow perhaps?

DAY FOUR

Step 8   Define Your Dollars II
(Day 4: Implement)

Day 4
Easy Action Steps (Recap)

Step 8 Define Your Dollars (implement)
Re-read this step and plan a day to implement it.

- Open 3 checking accounts within the same bank for free and easy transfers
- **Deposit Account** (where all your money lands and should be the account linked to your debit card and where your cash account / allowance is held), **Bills Account, Emergency Account** (for minor emergency)
- Open a Long Term Savings Account (or money market account) and link it to your Deposit Account
- Use sites like bankrate.com to choose the best bank for your Long Term Savings Account
- If available, sign up for direct deposit via your job, online banking and bill pay (even if you choose to pay the bills yourself rather than letting companies come in to take their payments). Decide how much of your New Savings you want to allocate to your Emergency Account and how much to your Long Term Savings Account.
- Automate your transfers from your Deposit Account to Bills, Emergency Savings and Long Term Savings
- Automate your bill payments
- Buy with CASH!!

I know this seems like a laundry list of things, but it really is not a lot to do. You can organize your money by opening multiple accounts. These accounts will help simplify your financial life and save you time and money. I assure you it is much easier than foreclosing on your home, getting evicted or having your car repossessed. Ultimately, the choice is yours. I can only make suggestions based on my successful experiences and of those whom I have helped. But remember, "If you always do what you've always done, you'll always get what you've always got!" Try a new system of managing your finances, adopt new habits, and I guarantee you will see a positive difference in your financial life.

To make things easier, I have provided a blank *Account Information Sheet* (provided on the next page). Use it to keep a record of all of your accounts. There is a place provided for the name of the account, the account number, user ID/ password, the due date (if there is one) and important info such as: interest rate, contact info/phone numbers. I keep a list like this in my office, it makes it easier when you have to call about a certain account. You will no longer have to toss papers around looking for your account information; it's now all in one place.

ACCOUNT INFORMATION

NAME	ACCOUNT NUMBER	USER ID / PASSWORD	DUE DATE	OTHER INFORMATION

DAY FIVE

Step 9   The Budget Grid

Step 9
The Budget Grid

It is your work to clear away the mass of encumbering material of thoughts, so that you may bring into plain view the precious thing at the center of the mass.
– Robert Collier (best-selling self-help book author)

Let's get organized!
– Me (The Budgetnista)

Giving until it Hurts

I met Adaeze at the Women's Self Empowerment Luncheon I mentioned earlier. She sat next to me and we struck up a conversation and was pleasantly surprised when she found out that I was one of the invited speakers. She was even more excited when I told her I was speaking about financial empowerment. Adaeze was born in Africa, and came to the United States to pursue the wide range of opportunities the country offers. Like many in her position, she was sending a lot of money and aid back to her family in Africa. The day we met, she took my card and promised to contact me right away, and she did.

I found Adaeze to be a soft spoken and gentle woman, who had trouble denying her family, even though it was putting a strain on her own finances. During our first meeting, I noticed that she had two new laptop computers that she was planning to ship home to Africa. After reviewing her finances, I found that not only could she not afford the computer, she needed to reduce the amount of money she sent to her family until she was financially able. I could tell that she felt very uncomfortable with my assessment of her financial situation.

As you know from my intro in the beginning of the book (I hope you didn't skipped it!), I too am African (and American) so I can fully appreciate how Adaeze felt about helping her family abroad. In many cultures, it is considered your duty to help those you left behind in your pursuit of a better life. If there are those who sacrificed to help make your dreams possible, it is only right to help them in return. I spent my whole life proudly watching my parents help our family members both here and in Nigeria. After seeing Adaeze's reaction to my assessment of her finances, I shared with her some wise advice that my father shared with me about giving, "You never give more than you are able to give."

Adaeze was giving more than she had. The hard truth was she was behind on many of her bills and was not able to afford some of her basic necessities. She would never catch up if she continued giving away so much money. After completing Step 1 through Step 8, we began to set up her Budget Grid (Step 9). The purpose of a Budget Grid is to provide the user with a way to quickly and efficiently see their expenses, the amounts and when they are due. With the help of the Budget Grid, Adeze was able to create a financial plan. This plan showed that with a second job, a raise, or an increase in income through a new job, she would be able to adequately manage her finances as well as help her family.

I am blessed to have an extensive group of family, friends and acquaintances. So when Adaeze mentioned one of the agencies she had applied to work for, I told her my friend Carol happened to work for that agency as well. I called Carol and she was generous enough to give Adaeze the direct number to the hiring coordinator. I believe that with her financial plan in place, Adaeze will be able to fulfill the dream that originally brought her to the United States.

A Visual Picture
It is your turn to create your own Budget Grid. Now that you have separated and reduced your expenses (Steps 4 and 5), have a newly revamped Money List (Steps 6 and 7) and have opened extra bank accounts (Step 8), we can create a Budget Grid that will help you maintain a watchful eye over your finances (Step 9). If you are truly serious about improving your finances, you need to see how your money is working...a visual picture.

You can do this with a pen and paper or spreadsheets. For now, use the blank template that's provided after Day 5 Easy Action Steps. In an effort to go green, I recommend using a computer spreadsheet in the future. This way, you will be able to make quick changes without having to rewrite your grid each time.

When creating your Budget Grid, remember to pay yourself first in the form of savings. It should be your number one priority and placed at the top of your list. Here is the format you should follow:

Six columns in your Budget Grid:

1) Account Name
2) Due Date
3) Name & Confirmation Number
4) Estimated Amount
5) Paid Amount
6) Date Paid

1) In the **Account Name column**, place *one* of the five accounts that you should now have opened: the *Deposit Account, Bills Account, Emergency Account, Long Term Savings Account* and good, old *Cash.* The primary role of this column is to be a placeholder for the names of the accounts where you want your money to be allocated and held.

2) The **Due Date column** is where you put the due dates of all your expenses, even your savings. This will help you to know at a glance when things need to be paid. Everything you spend money on should have a date associated with it. If it does not, decide for yourself what the date should be.

3) The **Name and Confirmation Number column** is self-explanatory. Place the name of the creditor and if you receive one after making a bill payment, place the confirmation number here too. This is for your records.

4) The **Estimated Amount column** is where you will place the estimated or the average amount of a pending bill or expense (use your *What You Could Spend Now* amounts from Step 7, from your revamped Money List). This is done to get you in the habit of pre-paying your expenses and bills to yourself in your *Bills Account.* By setting aside money for anticipated bills, you will be able to stop robbing Peter to pay Paul. Scrambling to get your bills paid on time will no longer be an issue. If you overestimate more than what your expenses actually end up costing you, take what you need from the *Emergency Account* (don't forget you have to pay it back). If you underestimate, you can leave the extra money into your *Bills Account* for financial cushion, or you can use the money to pay back your *Emergency Account.* Do you see the importance these extra accounts have in your financial management? Each account will play a role and every penny will have a place.

5) The **Paid Amount column** is another self-explanatory column. This column should only be filled in with the corresponding amount when you actually pay the expense.

6) The **Date Paid column** is for your record-keeping purposes. This column should be filled in with the date on which the expense was *actually* paid.

Take a look at Bella's Budget Grid on the next page; she was shocked at how quickly she was able to get organized. Use her grid to help you fill out yours. Continue reading, but don't forget I provided a blank Budget Grid template for you afterDay 5 Easy Action Steps.

 Quick Tip: If you are single, it may not be necessary to detail all of your cash items. Simply tally them up and lump them together. Then label them as *All Cash Items* on your budget grid. For those of you who are married, and especially if you have children, keeping your cash items itemized is beneficial. It provides you with a clear spending plan that is essential for successful family budgeting.

Study both of Bella's Step 9 examples, then choose which way best suits you, cash items combined or separated.

Bella's Step 9 example: The Budget Grid (with cash items separated)

MONTHLY TAKE HOME PAY	$3,700.00				
ACCOUNT	DUE DATE	NAME & CONFIRMATION #	ESTIMATED AMOUNT	AMOUNT PAID	DATE PAID
Long term Savings	1st & 15th/20__	Long term Savings	$215.00	$	
Emergency Savings	1st/ & 15th/20__	Emergency Savings	$120.00	$	
Bills	/1/20__	RENT	$750.00	$	
Bills	/19/20__	CELL PHONE	$45.00	$	
Bills	/7/20__	CREDIT CARDS	$175.00	$	
Bills	/23/20__	CAR NOTE	$450.00	$	
Bills	/4/20__	CAR INSURANCE	$275.00	$	
Bills	/18/20__	OFFERING/CHARITY	$30.00	$	
Bills	/3/20__	GAS AND ELECTRIC	$90.00	$	
Bills	/17/20__	CABLE	$50.00	$	
Bills	/17/20__	PHONE	$30.00	$	
Bills	/17/20__	INTERNET	$30.00	$	
Bills	/5/20__	LOANS	$150.00	$	
Cash/Allowance	1st & 15th/ 20__	BREAKFAST	$50.00	$	
Cash	1st & 15th/ 20__	LAUNDRY	$30.00	$	
Cash	1st & 15th/ 20__	CLOTHES	$50.00	$	
Cash	1st & 15th/ 20__	FOOD/GROCERIES	$375.00	$	
Cash	1st & 15th/ 20__	GROOMING	$100.00	$	
Cash	1st & 15th/ 20__	CHILD EXPENSES	$300.00	$	
Cash	1st & 15th/ 20__	TOILETRIES	$85.00	$	
Cash	1st & 15th/ 20__	LUNCH	$50.00	$	
Cash	1st & 15th/ 20__	ENTERTAINMENT	$75.00	$	
Cash	1st & 15th/ 20__	GAS (CAR)	$175.00	$	
TOTAL			$3,700.00	$	

Bella's Step 9 example: The Budget Grid (with combined cash items)

MONTHLY TAKE HOME PAY	$3,700.00				
ACCOUNT	DUE DATE	NAME & CONFIRMATION #	ESTIMATED AMOUNT	AMOUNT PAID	DATE PAID
Long term Savings	1st & 15th/ 20__	Long term Savings	$215.00	$	
Emergency Savings	1st & 15th/ 20__	Emergency Savings	$120.00	$	
Bills	/1/20__	RENT	$750.00	$	
Bills	/19/20__	CELL PHONE	$45.00	$	
Bills	/7/20__	CREDIT CARDS	$175.00	$	
Bills	/23/20__	CAR NOTE	$450.00	$	
Bills	/4/20__	CAR INSURANCE	$275.00	$	
Bills	/18/20__	OFFERING/CHARITY	$30.00	$	
Bills	/3/20__	GAS AND ELECTRIC	$90.00	$	
Bills	/17/20__	CABLE	$50.00	$	
Bills	/17/20__	PHONE	$30.00	$	
Bills	/17/20__	INTERNET	$30.00	$	
Bills	/5/20__	LOANS	$150.00	$	
Cash/ Allowance	1st & 15th/ 20__	ALL CASH ITEMS	$1,290.00	$	
TOTAL			$3,700.00	$	

Day 5
Easy Action Steps (Recap)

Step 9 The Budget Grid

- Fill out your own Budget Grid by first taking out your revamped Money List from Step 7.
- Transfer the names of the your expenses from your revamped Money List to the Name & Confirmation column on your Budget Grid blank template. *Long Term Savings* and *Emergency Savings* should be first since savings is a high priority expense.
- Decide how you will split your savings between these two accounts and fill in the *Long Term Savings, Emergency Savings Account* name and *Estimated Amounts.*

 Tip: Don't forget, you should strive to have at least 3 months to 2 year's worth of savings in the Long Term Savings Account. This account should also include any other long-term goal money you might want to house there.

- Transfer your *What You Could Spend* amounts from Step 7 to the *Estimated Amount* column on your Budget Grid.
- Next, fill out the Due Date column. If the expense has no due date (like cash/ allowance), create one. I use to pay myself a cash allowance twice a month, on the first and the fifteenth. I've since taken it a step further and divide the payments in two for a weekly allowance. It's ok to copy off of me and do the same (as a teacher it felt weird condoning copying).
- Look at your Name and Confirmation Number column and decide in which account the money you use to pay for this expense will be housed. Then, write one of the five account names (*Deposit, Bills, Emergency Savings, Long Term Savings and Cash*) in the Account column your Budget Grid.

 Tip: You may not use the Deposit Account in this column since money is rarely stored here. However, it is transferred from here to other accounts.

- Leave Paid Amount and Date Paid blank. Those columns should only be filled in after you or the bank actually pays the expense.

 Tip: Group your expenses together by account name on your Budget Grid (Deposit, Bills, Emergency Savings, Long Term Savings and Cash). This will make it easier to see where your money is and keep you more organized. Use Bella's Budget Grid examples from this step to help you.

- Last, fill in your *Monthly Take Home Pay* at the top of your grid.

Your blank Budget Grid awaits...

Blank template for Step 9

MONTHLY TAKE HOME PAY	$				
ACCOUNT	DUE DATE	NAME & CONFIRMATION	ESTIMATED AMOUNT	AMOUNT PAID	DATE PAID
			$	$	
			$	$	
			$	$	
			$	$	
			$	$	
			$	$	
			$	$	
			$	$	
			$	$	
			$	$	
			$	$	
			$	$	
			$	$	
			$	$	
			$	$	
			$	$	
			$	$	
			$	$	
			$	$	
			$	$	
			$	$	
			$	$	
			$	$	
			$	$	
			$	$	
			$	$	
TOTAL			$	$	

NOTES:

DAY SIX

Step 10   Separate Your Budget Grid

Step 10
Separate Your Budget Grid

Divide your movements into easy-to-do sections. If you fail, divide again.
– Peter Nivio Zarlenga (author)

A Home of My Own
In 2004, I was 24 years old. My sister/roomate and I had been living away from our parents for about a year and a half. By raising the rent, the woman who owned the home we lived in inspired my goal of homeownership. However, it would take almost two years before my dream would come to fruition. During those two years, I fully immersed myself in the home buying process. I read every book I could get my hands on, searched the Internet for hours and took a first-time-home-buyer's course and interviewed homeowners that I knew.

It was while taking the course that I fully came to appreciate my money management system. A gentleman named Basil French (not his real name, but oddly similar) facilitated the 4-week course. Basil was an excellent teacher. He provided the participants with a comprehensive overview about what was needed in order to successfully buy and keep your home. One of the stipulations for receiving the course's certificate was to produce a budget that illustrated your money management skills over a three-month span. By that time, I had been using a version of my budgeting system for almost four years. Before turning in my budget to Basil, I decided to separate my Budget Grid into two sections in order to make it easier for him to read and understand.

After that experience, I found that having two separate Budget Grids per month helped to further simplify my system. In an effort to pay your bills in a timely manner and track your spending, I recommend that you separate your Budget Grid into two pay periods. This will help you conveniently pay your bills twice a month. So create your Budget Grids according to the billing schedule of your expenses. This process may alleviate some of the confusion of maintaining a monthly budget. By separating it, you can focus on each grid accordingly as well as anticipate upcoming spending.

Change is Gonna Come
I know that many of you currently use the first check of the month to pay for bills due between the 1st and the 14th of that same month. What I am trying to introduce to you may be a new concept, but it is time to change your mindset. Start planning to pay your bills (into your *Bills Account*) a half a month ahead of time. Before we start, I know that many of you may be saying, "But I don't currently have the funds to set aside half a month's worth of bill money." Not to worry. I have some tips on how to do so (naturally). Finish reading this section on what to do with your money and I promise I'll teach you how to jumpstart the system later.

Even though I know you don't receive paper checks any longer because you have direct deposit, right? I will be using the word check to represent all income earned from your J-O-B (s). It may seem like the One Week Budget system is tailored for those who get paid biweekly or twice a month. Not true! Even if you get paid weekly (yeah!) or monthly (boo!), you can still use this system. For the ultra-lucky weekly folks, put two checks on one grid. For you unfortunate monthly folks, divide your check in half and put half the amount you earn each month on each Budget Grid. See? Problem solved!

Here's how you implement your better, brighter, paying-your-bills-on-time future. The first check(s) of this month (payments received between the 1st -14th) should pay for the second half of this month's expenses (expenses due between the 15th-31st) and be on budget Grid 1. The second check(s) of this month (payments received between the 15th – 31st) should pay for the 1st half of the next month's expenses (expenses due between the 1st – 14th of next month) and be on Budget Grid 2. By doing this, you will ensure that you will always have the money available to make timely bill payments. It will also give you a half a month's worth of cushion, should your paycheck ever come late or not at all (believe me I've been there).

So, whatever bills you want to pay or prepay between the 1st and 14th of each month will be on Budget Grid #2. The bills that you want to pay or prepay between the 15th and 31st of each month, will be put on Budget Grid #1. When you set up your budget grid, you may need to split some of your larger expenses in half, like your mortgage, rent or car payments. How often you need the money for a particular expense will also play a role in its placement on your grids. For example, you will more than likely pay for items with cash during the first and second half of the month. With that said, you will need cash from each grid, so split your monthly cash in half and place the line item, ½ ALL CASH ITEMS, on both of your Budget Grids (for those of you single people who consolidated your cash account items). If you decide to take your cash allowance weekly, still maintain ½ ALL CASH ITEMS on each Budget Grid. Just make sure that you put two dates paid on each grid after taking your allowance each week.

The total of each Budget Grid (this will include your savings) should equal half of one month's pay. That is because each grid represents a half a month's expenses. For example, if your monthly income is $3,700 (like Bella's), each grid should equal half of that. That would be $1,850 or one check if you get paid twice a month. So when creating your grids, be sure to double check and make sure that each grid is balanced and adds up to ½ a month's pay.

For some, balancing your Budget Grids may take a little time, practice and patience. After separating your bills by due date, you may find that each grid does not add up to half of your monthly earnings. If this is the case, you have a few options to help make them balance.

1) Divide some of your larger bills in half and place that money into your *Bills Account* until they are actually due. As you will see in Bella's Step 10 example, she has divided her rent and car insurance in half. This means with each grid she's contributing to that upcoming expense.

2) Change the due dates of some of your expenses. If you compare Bella's Budget Grid in Step 9 to her second Budget Grid in the Step 10 example, you will notice that Bella changed the due date of her offering/charity expense from the 18th to the 13th of the month. There are some expenses for which you can choose their due dates. So change the date to make them fit into whatever Budget Grid you need them to fall under.

3) Finally, use your *Emergency Savings Account* or *Long Term Savings Account* to balance out your grids. Bella allocated a total of $120 to her *Emergency Savings Account* as a buffer for unexpected expenses or emergencies each month. At first, her Budget Grids did not equal $1850 (half of $3700), so she put $87 in her *Emergency Account* in Budget Grid #1 and $33 to Budget Grid #2, totaling $120 for the month to make the grids equal. You will have to play around with your numbers to make them reflect their appropriate amounts. Remember the totals from both grids should be the same.

This is an eye-opening experience you will only have to do one time. Once you automate it, you won't have to worry about paying bills again! Well maybe not EVER again, but you catch my drift. Another great perk is that you can use this system for the rest of your life! Please, do not let fear or laziness be the reason you continue to struggle financially, I cannot stress this enough.

Now it's your turn. But before using the blank Budget Grids I provided, study Bella's Budget Grid examples on the following pages first. Yes, I said study!

 Tip: Bella likes to add up her bills on each grid and put the Bill Total at the bottom of her Budget Grids (show off). It makes it easier to see how much money she will be transferring to her Bills account. I suggest you follow her lead.

Bella's Step 10 example: Separate Your Budget Grid: 1
(income received between the 1st – 14th, bills due between the 15th – 31st of this month)

MONTH you're paid in:	January				
TOTAL TAKE HOME PAY	$1,850.00				
TAKE HOME PAY	$1,850.00				
SOURCE	Primary Job				
Date:	January/1st – 14th/ 20__				
ACCOUNT	DUE DATE	NAME & CONFIRMATION #	ESTIMATED AMOUNT	AMOUNT PAID	DATE PAID
Long term Savings	1/15/20__	Long Term Savings	$0.00	$	
Emergency Savings	1/15/20__	Emergency Savings	$87.00	$	
Bills	2/1/20__	½ FEBUARY RENT (1)	$375.00	$	
Bills	1/23/20__	CAR NOTE	$450.00	$	
Bills	2/4/20__	½ FEB.CAR INSURANCE	$138.00	$	
Bills	1/17/20__	CABLE	$50.00	$	
Bills	1/17/20__	PHONE	$30.00	$	
Bills	1/19/20__	CELL PHONE	$45.00	$	
Bills	1/17/20__	INTERNET	$30.00	$	
Cash	1/15/20__	½ CASH	$645.00	$	
BILL TOTAL			$1,118.00	$	
TOTAL			$1,850.00	$	

 Note: If you've split a large bill in half (like rent and car insurance) and it appears on both grids, that date may not fall between the 15th – 31st on this grid.

Bella's Step 10 example: Separate Your Budget Grid: 2
(income received between the 15th – 31st, bills due between the 1st – 14th of next month)

MONTH you're paid in:	January				
TOTAL TAKE HOME PAY	$1,850.00				
TAKE HOME PAY	$1,850.00				
SOURCE	Primary Job				
Date:	January/15th- 31st /20__				
ACCOUNT	DUE DATE	NAME & CONFIRMATION #	ESTIMATED AMOUNT	AMOUNT PAID	DATE PAID
Long term Savings	2/1/20__	Long Term Savings	$215.00	$	
Emergency Savings	2/1/20__	Emergency Savings	$33.00	$	
Bills	2/1/20__	½ FEBUARY RENT (2)	$375.00	4	
Bills	2/7/20__	CREDIT CARDS	$175.00	4	
Bills	2/4/20__	½ FEB CAR INSURANCE	$137.00	$	
Bills	2/3/20__	GAS AND ELECTRIC	$90.00	$	
Bills	2/5/20__	LOANS	$150.00	$	
Bills	2/13/20__	OFFERING/ CHARITY	$30.00	$	
Cash	2/1/20__	½ CASH	$645.00	$	
BILL TOTAL			$957.00	$	
TOTAL			$1,850.00	$	

Once again take note of how the check received in the first half of January is paying for the second half of January's expenses and the second half of January is paying for the first half of February's expenses. Now you are ready to do it yourself. Your blank Budget Grid template awaits after Day 6 Easy Action Steps. Just think, one more day left to making a permanent positive change in your financial future forever....

Day 6
Easy Action Steps (Recap)

Step 10 Separate Your Budget Grids
- Place all income received between the 1st – 14th and all bills due between the 15th – 31st on Budget Grid 1. Be sure to include all the information for the bills: account, due date, name and estimated amount.
- Place all income received between the 15th – 31st and all bills due between the 1st – 14th on Budget Grid 2. Be sure to include all info for the bills: account, due date, name and estimated amount.
- Both Budget Grid's Totals must equal each other and half a month's income. They must be balanced, unless you receive additional income from another source outside of your primary job.

Balance Tips
- Divide larger bills in half (i.e. rent, mortgage). Place half the amount of the divided bill on each of the budget grids. Don't forget that the due date will be the same on both grids.
- Change the due dates of the expenses you control (i.e. charity).
- Use your Long Term and Emergency Savings to balance your grid. For example, you might place 20% of your savings on one grid and 80% on another.
- Always split Cash in half and place the amount on each grid. This way you will receive spending money at least twice a month. I bet you never thought you'd be getting allowance again?

Your turn! Fill in your blank Budget Grid templates on the next two pages.

Blank templates for Step 10

BUDGET GRID 1
(income received between the 1st – 14th, bills due between the 15th – 31st of this month)

MONTH:					
TOTAL TAKE HOME PAY	$				
TAKE HOME PAY AMT:	$				
SOURCE					
Date:					
ACCOUNT	DUE DATE	NAME & CONFIRMATION #	ESTIMATED AMOUNT	AMOUNT PAID	DATE PAID
			$	$	
			$	$	
			$	$	
			$	$	
			$	$	
			$	$	
			$	$	
			$	$	
			$	$	
			$	$	
			$	$	
			$	$	
			$	$	
BILL TOTAL			$	$	
TOTAL			$	$	

BUDGET GRID 2
(income received between the 15th – 31st, bills due between the 1st – 14th of next month)

MONTH:					
TOTAL TAKE HOME PAY	$				
TAKE HOME PAY AMT:	$				
SOURCE					
Date:					
ACCOUNT	DUE DATE	NAME & CONFIRMATION #	ESTIMATED AMOUNT	AMOUNT PAID	DATE PAID
			$	$	
			$	$	
			$	$	
			$	$	
			$	$	
			$	$	
			$	$	
			$	$	
			$	$	
			$	$	
			$	$	
			$	$	
			$	$	
BILL TOTAL			$	$	
TOTAL			$	$	

(Extra blank copies in the Appendix)

Quick Tip: Tally up your bills amount at the bottom of each budget grid. This way, you will know how much your total biweekly bill amount is at a glance. Make and keep copies of your budget template. Better yet, green it out and create a spreadsheet on your computer. By doing this, you won't have to create them every month. Just fill out the AMOUNT PAID and DATE PAID every two weeks. I do this, and that's why it takes me less than 30 minutes each month to manage my day-to-day money.

DAY SEVEN

Step 11
Prepay Bills

The early bird catches the worm.
- Unknown

Life is all about timing.
– Stacey Charter (cancer survivor, divorce survivor, attack survivor)

The Early Bird
One of my sisters (I will not say which one) is notorious for pre-paying her bills. At times, she is months ahead of schedule! Don't worry! I am not suggesting that you go to that extreme. The reason for her pre-paying ways is that she works in an industry that has proven to be unstable at times. This instability stems from constant bad publicity and high profile lawsuits (the industry, not her). By pre-paying expenses to herself or to the companies she owes, she has been able to survive the turbulent times without suffering financially.

Pre-paying bills is another form of emergency savings. Having funds set aside for bills in advance will help eliminate a lot of money-related stress. Another benefit of pre-paying your bills is increasing and/or maintaining your credit score. 35% of your credit score depends on your ability to pay debts on time. I know that pre-paying bills may sound a little strange to those of you who enjoy the rush of late payments and the fees associated with them. I'm not pointing any fingers...

Ahead of the Game
To reduce your risk of falling behind in your bills, I suggest prepaying your bills to yourself first. How? You can do this by setting aside the money in your *Bills Account* before they are due. One of the purposes of Step 10 (Separate your Budget Grids) was for you to be able to see how much money you need to deposit in your *Bills Account* bi-weekly. Although your bills are due on different days throughout the month, you now only have to pay them twice a month to yourself! Let your automatic bill payment worry about the actual due dates. And if for some reason you become unemployed or stop receiving money, you have a little time to adjust without worrying about how you will pay for your immediate upcoming expenses. This is because you will have already set aside the next two weeks worth of bill money in your *Bills Account*.

Step 11 is where the *Estimated Amount* column will come in handy. By now, you know about how much your expenses will cost well before your bills are even due. You also understand that paying your bills into your *Bills Account* ensures that the money is always ready and available. The larger the bill, the earlier it should be pre-paid to you. By doing so, you will give yourself some time to recover if you should ever lose your income. Not only should you pre-pay your bills to yourself, but you should pre-pay your bills to your creditors and stop waiting until the last minute. There is nothing wrong with sending your money to them a week in advance. By doing this, your account will always remain in good standing. If by chance a mistake is made (like a lost payment), you will have a week to make sure it is corrected.

As promised here are some ways you can get the funds to set aside half a month's worth of bill money.

- Use your tax refund check. As tax season approaches, make up your mind to use your money wisely. You now know how much half a month's worth of bills costs you. If you get a refund, pay those bills off! That way, you can stash your upcoming check to pay for the next half of the month's bills. Voila!

 Sidenote: If you are receiving a very large refund every year, you are giving the government an interest free loan. Ask your HR department about how you can receive a larger pay check now, verses a larger refund later.

- There is a little known perk for us folks who get paid bi-weekly. Twice a year, usually in the fall and summer, we get three checks in a month. I know you're smiling while reading this, if this happens to you. I suggest that you use the extra check during those months to turbo boost your budget. Pay bills ahead of time and put yourself half a month ahead.

- Lastly, yet a little less glamorous and expedient, save up some of your new-found savings and pre-pay your bills that way.

thebudgetnista.biz

Step 12
Work the System

It pays to plan ahead. It wasn't raining when Noah built the ark.
- Unknown

He who fails to plan, plans to fail.
- A proverb

A good plan today is better than a perfect plan tomorrow.
- A proverb

Good but not Great

If holding yourself financially accountable is new to you, then budgeting may take some getting used to. Once you learn to work the system and tailor it to your needs, you'll never look at your personal finances the same way again. One of my first clients, Selena is a great example of this.

Selena was 25 when I met her. She wasn't a careless spender, nor was she a careful saver. Selena paid her bills on time and saved a little cash each month, but just like me and many of you, she wasn't satisfied with the state of her finances. She knew there had to be a better way. Selena embraced the system wholeheartedly and even suggested beneficial changes that I have since implemented. Within four months of using the One Week Budget system, Selena went from having $1,000 in the bank to having $8,000. The $8000 was a combination of her current savings, a tax refund and her new monthly savings.

How Selena saved $8000 in four months:

Tax refund	$3000
New monthly savings ($1000x 4months)	$4000
Current savings	$1000
Total	$8000 ☺

Here's how she did it: Selena created her Money List **(Step1)**, inputted her monthly amounts **(Step 2)**, calculated her Beginning Savings **(Step 3)**, separated her expenses **(Step 4)**, reduced her spending **(Step 5)**, determined her New Savings amount, $1000 **(Step 6)**, revamped her Money List to reflect the changes made **(Step 7)**, defined her dollars by opening up the necessary accounts **(Step 8)**, created and separated her Budget Grids **(Step 9** and **10)**, prepaid her bills **(Step 11)**, and truly worked the system **(Step 12)**.

Sidenote: Selena reduced her spending by cutting excessive eating out, reduced shopping, cutting entertainment spending and lowering her cable bill.

One of the most important lessons I learned from Selena was that everyone's approach to money is different. There is no *one* way of handling one's personal finances. With the *One Week Budget*, I have strived to give you a flexible template for personal money management that can be easily implemented within a short period of time. For the last 10 years, I have used this system and have seen how it has financially empowered people to help themselves. It is up to you to take action and modify The One Week Budget to fit your own needs. I know it feels like we are family now, but you won't hurt my feelings if you alter my steps to make them work for you.

If you do complete each step (or your own version of them), learn to work the system using your own rhythm. Remember, it is not how much you make, it's how you manage it that separates the haves from the have-nots.

Day 7
Easy Action Steps (Recap)

Step 11   Prepay Bills
Step 12   Work the System

You are finally at the end of your journey, so give yourself a pat on the back! For those less flexible folks, give yourself a hug. Now that you have made it through each step successfully, I want to give you a brief outline of how to actually work this system.

- Allocate **at least** 10% of your gross income (income before taxes and deductions) to a retirement account (ask your employer, financial advisor or local bank for more information).
- All money earned should first be deposited into the *Deposit Account*.
- Transfer funds from your *Deposit Account* to your *Long Term Savings* and *Emergency Account*. **Automate the transfers**.
- Tally up your Bill Total amounts every other week and transfer the amount from your *Deposit Account* to your *Bills Account*. This is how you **prepay your bills** (Step 11). **Automate the transfers**.
- Take out your allocated cash (*Cash Account*) from your *Deposit Account* as needed. This is your bi-weekly allowance (as you already know, I break it down even further and give myself a small allowance each week –total monthly cash divided by four weeks).
- AUTOMATE, AUTOMATE, AUTOMATE your *Long Term Savings, Emergency Savings*, bill payments and transfers from your *Deposit Account*.
- Fill out the Amount Paid and Date Paid columns bi-monthly as you pay each expense.
- Most importantly: just because you have an automated system, it doesn't mean you do not have to check it from time to time. The purpose of the Amount Paid and Date Paid portion of your Budget Grid is to force you to physically manage your money at least twice a month. It also forces you to maintain a tangible record of your finances. I can tell you from firsthand experience, that if you skip the record-keeping step of this system, you WILL lose more money than you can shake a stick at. I know, because I've shaken a lot of sticks!

 Sidenote: You'll see how useful this system is when you do your taxes this year. Believe me, you will thank me.

As you read on, you will find examples of Bella's two fully-completed Budget Grids. Here are several things to note:

- The space provided for additional income: If you receive income from more than one source, you must make note of it on your grid. To do this, add up all additional income and place it by *Total Take Home Pay.* Your total take home pay should always equal the *Total* at the bottom of your grid. Bear in mind that if you do receive another source of income your *Total Take Home Pay* may not be the same on both grids.
- The word PAID in the right hand corner: Only place PAID here when both the amount paid and date paid columns are completely filled. This is so that when you look back at previous grids, you'll know right away if you have any outstanding, unpaid expenses. Once again, *Total Take Home Pay* should reflect all income earned during that half of the month.
- Lastly, if you receive an unexpected bill that is not part of your normal monthly rotation, don't forget to place it on one of the Budget Grids.
- You have to account for all of your expenses and spending.

Bella's Step 12 example: Work the System, Budget Grid 1

MONTH you're paid:	January				PAID
TOTAL TAKE HOME PAY	$1,850.00				
TAKE HOME PAY AMT.	$1,850.00	$			
SOURCE	Primary Job	Additional Income			
Date:	January/1st – 14th/ 20__				
ACCOUNT	DUE DATE	NAME & CONFIRMATION #	ESTIMATED AMOUNT	AMOUNT PAID	DATE PAID
Long term Savings	1/15/20__	Long Term Savings	$0.00	$0.00	1/15/20__
Emergency Savings	1/15/20__	Emergency Savings	$87.00	$87.00	1/15/20__
Bills	2/1/20__	½ FEBRUARY RENT (1)	$375.00	$375.00	2/1/20__
Bills	1/23/20__	CAR NOTE	$450.00	$450.00	1/23/20__
Bills	2/4/20__	½ FEB.CAR INSURANCE	$138.00	$138.00	2/4/20__
Bills	1/17/20__	CABLE	$50.00	$50.00	1/17/20__
Bills	1/17/20__	PHONE	$30.00	$30.00	1/17/20__
Bills	1/19/20__	CELL PHONE	$45.00	$45.00	1/19/20__
Bills	1/17/20__	INTERNET	$30.00	$30.00	1/17/20__
Cash	1/15/20__	½ CASH	$645.00	$645.00	1/15/20__
BILL TOTAL			$1,118.00		
TOTAL			$1,850.00		

Bella's Step 12 example: Work the System, Budget Grid 2

MONTH you're paid:	January				PAID
TOTAL TAKE HOME PAY	$1,850.00				
TAKE HOME PAY AMT.	$1,850.00	$			
SOURCE	Primary Job	Additional Income			
Date:	January/15th-31st /20__				
ACCOUNT	DUE DATE	NAME & CONFIRMATION #	ESTIMATED AMOUNT	AMOUNT PAID	DATE PAID
Long term Savings	2/1/20__	Long Term Savings	$215.00	$215.00	
Emergency Savings	2/1/20__	Emergency Savings	$33.00	$33.00	
Bills	2/1/20__	½ FEBRUARY RENT (2)	$375.00	$375.00	
Bills	2/7/20__	CREDIT CARDS	$175.00	$175.00	
Bills	2/4/20__	½ FEB CAR INSURANCE	$137.00	$137.00	
Bills	2/3/20__	GAS AND ELECTRIC	$90.00	$90.00	
Bills	2/5/20__	LOANS	$150.00	$150.00	
Bills	2/13/20__	OFFERING/ CHARITY	$30.00	$30.00	
Cash	2/1/20__	½ CASH	$645.00	$645.00	
BILL TOTAL			$957.00	$957.00	
TOTAL			$1,850.00	$1,850.00	

See how Bella's *Totals* on both Budget Grids equal to half of a month's pay? (This includes all income made in half a month.) Your budget grids must do the same unless you have a second source of additional income that you received. Step 12 puts you over the finish line! You are now ready to incorporate **The One Week Budget** into your life. It has been a long journey for some, but well worth it. Physically it's been seven days, but mentally you know it's been years.

I cannot stress this enough: if you automate everything, your only (but extremely important) responsibility will be to check to make sure all of your transfers went through. You also have to check that your bills were paid as specified. The purpose of the Budget Grids is for you to keep a physical record of your automated finances (in the Amount Paid and Date Paid columns).

I update my grids every other Saturday morning. It takes me about fifteen minutes to complete the process. Imagine being in full fiscal control of your day-to-day finances and spending only thirty minutes a *month* doing so! Take a breath of fresh air! You are now financially organized. Welcome to the frugal yet fabulous world of **The One Week Budget**!

Remember, to give is to receive. Give and live life generously. Generosity breeds wealth (and I'm not just talking about money). Stay financially empowered!

NOTES:

BONUS CHAPTER

Debt & Credit

Bonus Chapter
Debt and Credit

Neither a borrower nor a lender be.
- Polonius (a character in Hamlet, a play by Shakespeare)

My Story
Many of you may now be under the impression that I'm amazingly witty (smile) and that I have always lived a financially responsible life. You'd be right, minus the always financially responsible part. I haven't always followed the basic money rules I write, speak and teach about. But making those costly mistakes have been both a blessing and a curse. A curse because, let's face it, who wants to lose money? It's a blessing because it has enabled me to write possibly the most important chapter in this book. This is a chapter that the majority of you will need to read, whether you like it or not. In keeping with the format of the book, I'll give you advice about debt and credit by illustrating it through a true story. . . my story. Light, camera, action! Cue dramatic introduction music (and just so you know, a younger Halle Berry plays me in my version).

Growing up, my mother and especially my father demanded that my sisters and I take responsibility for our actions. My father, an accountant, emphasized the importance of fiscal accountability. He openly discussed the family's finances with his girls (my four sisters and I). When we acquired our first jobs, he personally took us to the bank to open our first bank accounts.

I was raised to wisely manage my money and for the most part, I did. I never had a car note, always paid my bills in full and on time, saved excessively and NEVER, EVER carried a credit card balance. I got my first credit card when I was 18 because my Dad, in all of his wisdom, understood that an important part of having a strong credit score was the length of time one has actually had credit. There are five key components of a credit score and each component plays a weighted role in your financial future. The five components are: inquiries 10%, type of debt 10%, length of credit history 15%, debt-to-income ratio 30%, payment history 35%.

1) Inquiries 10%:
An inquiry happens when your credit report is looked up. Each time someone other than you requests your credit report, your score potentially goes down by 8-12 points. Sometimes, it is necessary to have your credit report pulled. For example, reports are requested when you apply for certain jobs, renting a car, getting car insurance, opening up a new credit card or applying for a loan. Remember to be careful when allowing someone to look up your credit. You maybe unnecessarily sacrificing credit score points.

2) Type of Debt 10%:

The three main Credit Bureaus, Equifax, Experian and TransUnion, like to see different *types* of debt. For example, if all you have are student loans, you look like an inexperienced debtor who may not be able to handle other kinds of debt (like, credit cards, a mortgage, or a car note). I'm not suggesting that you get into debt for debt sake. I just want you to be aware of what the credit bureaus look at when assigning you that all important number......your credit score.

3) Length of Credit History 15%:

The longer you've had your credit and have paid debts on time, the better. Be sure to keep that in mind when deciding whether or not to close a credit card. You may want to consider closing one of your newer cards instead. Your older cards are proof of a longer credit history, which helps you in the end.

4) Debt-to-Income Ratio 30%:

Your debt-to-income is the amount of income you receive, divided by the amount of debt you have. For example, if your monthly income is $10,000 before taxes (I wish) and monthly debt payments are $5,000 a month, your debt-to-income ratio would be 50%. The lower the ratio the better. 50% is too high! Lenders like to see a ratio between 20-25%. A ratio that is too high may mean you are unable to make consistent on time debt payments. The higher the ratio, the higher the interest rate you might be charged on your debt and no one likes that.

5) Payment History – 35%

This section of your credit report contains the bulk of the information. It includes all of your credit accounts and details about how you've paid them. The way you pay is rated from 1-9. The number 1 is the best (on time, good payment record), 9 is the worst (collections, judgments and other nasty items). The good thing is, over time and with consistent timely payments, you can raise this section within several months.

Now you know that even if you pay all of your bills on time, you still need to keep in mind the other aspects of your credit score. My father understood this, so to help me develop the length of my credit and payment history, he allowed me to open up an account while I was still a teenager. He allowed me to use the credit card for very small purchases each month (mostly gas) and then he paid the balance off in full each month. By doing this, he helped me build my credit history before I even understood what credit was! (Thanks Daddy!) He is one of the reasons I was able to purchase my first home at age 25. Although I had enough money saved (about $40,000) and I always paid my bills on time and in full, I had very little credit history. The fact that I could show my lender 7 years of responsible credit card usage (age 18-25) was one of the reasons I was approved for my home loan.

Disclaimer: I am not suggesting that you open up a credit card in your child's name so that you can build up his/her credit. My father is an extremely disciplined man. He did not allow me to abuse the card I got. As easy as it is to build your child's credit, it is even easier to destroy it. If you know that you are not making *on-time, full payments on your own credit card*, this is not for you or your child. I have had numerous friends who had terrible credit before they even reached high school. This was all because their parents had a lapse in judgment. They opened up cards in their children's name, but didn't maintain a good payment history. You don't want bill collectors calling your 10 year old. Believe me, I've seen it happen!

Back to my story...

Before I purchased my house, I created an airtight budget using the same One Week Budget system I just taught you (what's good for the goose....). My budget allowed me to make a seamless transition between renting and owning. It also allowed me to continue to contribute to my retirement fund, save cash every month and pay all of my bills (including my mortgage) on time and in full each month. Oh, and did I mention AUTOMATICALLY? Life was great and I became complacent and I'll admit, a little careless with my finances.

After living in my home for a couple of years, I decided that I wanted to take my money to another level. I contacted a wealthy friend and asked him to teach me about investing. He offered to help invest my money and I eagerly and stupidly accepted. One of the ways my friend made his income was by buying wholesale luxury retail and supplying the clothing to a network of stores overseas. After meeting with him several times, I decided to invest $20,000 (crazy, I know). In all of my infinite wisdom (sarcastically speaking), I decided not to use my savings, but to open up two credit cards and use the money from them instead (are you cringing yet?). The return, he promised me, was astronomical and was to be paid monthly over a two-year period. I was so confident that I would be hitting pay day soon, that I purchased a Financial Coaching System (a year's worth of weekly one-on-one sessions and corresponding material) from one of my favorite authors for $15,000 also on the credit card (have you passed out yet?)!

So let me break down my Financial Fiasco:
Tiffany's not-so-bright idea
2 credit cards
$20,000 invested with a 'friend'
$15,000 on financial coaching

$35, 000 Financial Fiasco

As you may have figued out, the deal with my friend fell through. He had a health emergency and was hospitalized for over a month. So his stores and suppliers moved on. I was now stuck with $35,000 worth of credit card debt, when I previously had none. At age 27, I had NEVER, EVER carried a balance on my credit card, let alone have more than one credit card open. Honestly, I didn't know what to do. So for a year, I did nothing. I just sat waiting for some miracle to happen and hoped my friend would get better and help me clean up the financial mess I created. I know by now you must have a million and one questions, so I'll try to answer some of them.

Why didn't you use the money in your bank account to invest?
I wanted to maintain my emergency money. It was also the summer and as a teacher I didn't work, so I also needed some money to support myself during my two months off.

Why didn't you pay off the credit card with your savings?
Another friend had a medical emergency and I let her borrow most of my non-summer savings. You won't believe how expensive healthcare is when you are not insured. I did all of this before I knew I was going to lose my invested money.

Why did you do something so stupid?
It seemed like a great idea at the time. Cliché? I know. I wanted to use the money I made to reinvest and eventually help my family here and abroad.

Just why?!
So I'd be inspired to write this chapter? Honestly, I really don't know. Maybe it was just error of my youth.

The Get Out Of Debt Plan
So what did I do? Well as previously stated, for about a year I did nothing. I wasn't struggling and I was paying more than the minimums on my credit card balances. I was still contributing to my retirement account, although I downgraded to 3% of my gross income, rather than 10%. I was still paying my bills on time and I was still saving cash each month (although, not much). My mortgage was always sitting in my bills account waiting to be automatically deducted so I was never in danger of losing my home. The silver lining on the dark cloud of my Financial Fiasco was that my One Week Budget system proved to be sound, even when I wasn't. It worked! It worked despite my time of poor financial decision making! It worked even as I remained financially frozen with fear. It worked when I needed it the most! It worked! It worked! It worked! There is no greater testament that I can give than that.

Looking back on the situation, I think the fact that I didn't feel like I was in dangerous financial trouble, was one of the reasons it took me a year to take action. As time went on, the heaviness of my credit card debt began to weigh on me. It was costing me a fortune and I hated only being able to save a little each month, especially toward retirement. I thought about my debt a lot and calculated that at the rate I was going, it would take a little over three years to pay it off. That was unacceptable.

The solution came to me one day, as it most often does. . . through someone I love, my sister (the one who pre-pays). She called to talk one day and ended up giving me great advice. She told me about this financial book she had just finished reading. In the book, the author advocated that the reader imagine their worst case financial scenario. Then, imagine what steps they would take to rectify the situation. Then he said, "Do it now! Don't wait until the worst case scenario happens!" If you are unhappy financially, you NEED to make big changes NOW. My sister then told me these words that helped change my life.

"If you're willing to live like no one else now, you will be able to live like no one else later."

Most people are unwilling to sacrifice to achieve their optimum existence. I prayed I wasn't like most people. That day I imagined my worst case scenario. It was losing my job and the threat of my home going into foreclosure. I then thought; if that happened, what would I do? I told myself, I'd move back home with Mommy and Daddy (yes, I still call them that) and live rent free for a year to get on my feet.

A month later I rented out my condo to a friend and then sold all of my furniture for more than I bought it for (what?!). I took the rest of my stuff and moved back home into my childhood room. My new tenant paid 90% of my mortgage, so I used the money I saved to expedite my no-more-credit-card-debt plan.

Next, I laid out my credit cards. At that time, I had four because I switched cards to take advantage of lower interest rates. Two of my cards had a 0% interest rate for six months. One of my cards maintained a 5% interest rate as long as I never used it again (this valuable information was all found in the small print portion of my credit card agreement, naturally). My oldest credit card, the one my dad had me open up had the highest rate, at 9%. I was tempted to close it but it was my oldest card and I needed it's longevity to help boost and maintain my credit score.

After laying out the cards it took me a couple of hours to calculate the best plan of action. I decided to pay off my credit cards based upon balances rather than interest rates. I chose to pay off the lowest balance first then the next lowest and so on. Some financial gurus may argue that it's best to pay off cards with the highest interest rates first. This method will help you save on interest, but I am an emotional person (clearly). I need to see progress right away to keep me motivated to stick to a plan. The best way for me to do this was by paying off the smaller debts first. So, I wrote down all of my credit card balances from lowest to highest, as well as their minimum monthly payments. I then calculated how much excess money I was now going to be able to save each month by moving home (my *New Savings*, Step 6): $1,500. I added this amount to the monthly minimum payment of my lowest credit card balance. Currently, you may be spreading your excess monthly money among whatever debt you may have. Stop and add up your excess money, then pay the minimum to all of your debt. Then choose which debt you will pay the minimum plus the excess money you've added up. Lastly, automate the payments.

Note: For the sake of simplicity, I did not factor in the effect of interest on the following pay-down-debt-system I will illustrate for you.

My Credit Card Debt Breakdown:

	Balance	Monthly Minimum Payment	Excess (New Savings)	Monthly Payment
1) Credit Card	$2,653.00	$70.00	$1,500.00	$1,570.00
2) Credit Card	$5,889.00	$123.00	$0.00	$123.00
3) Credit Card	$8,241.00	$115.00	$0.00	$115.00
4) Credit Card	$14,743.00	$227.00	$0.00	$227.00
Totals	$31,526.00	$535.00	$1,500.00	$2,035.00

As you can see by my credit card total, during my year of inaction, I was only able to lower my credit card debt from $35,000 to $31,526. You should also take note that I applied all of my excess money ($1500, New Savings) to credit card #1, the one with the lowest balance. In two months, I was able to pay off credit card # 1. Do the math. Credit Card #1's new payment amount was $1570 a month ($1500 + $70). $1570 multiplied by 2 (months) is $3140, $487 more than credit card #1's $2,653's balance. I was cooking with grease and I was only two months into my debt elimination plan!

I took the $487 left over from paying off credit card #1 and applied it to the balance on credit card #2. That card was now $5,643 because I paid the minimum ($123) on it for two months ($123 x 2= $246).

Credit Card #2 new balance breakdown

Original credit Card #2 balance	$5,889
Two months of minimum payments	-$246
Money left over from paying off credit card #1	-$487

Total balance left on credit card #2	**=$5156**

Do you realize that not only did I completely pay off one credit card in two months, but I also significantly lowered my second credit card balance as well? But, wait there's more.! Do you remember the original excess amount of money I was saving monthly by living at home? It was $1500, right? Do you also remember the minimum payment I was making on credit card #1? It was $70. I decided to add the $1500 and the $70 ($1,570) to the minimum of the second credit card which was $123. I was used to paying the $1570 each month and I didn't want to break my stride so I just put that monthly payment towards the next credit card (#2). That's a total of $1,693 ($1500+$70+$123) being applied to my newly lowered credit card #2's balance each month.

Next, I set up a new grid and put the new numbers I calculated into it.

	Balance	Monthly Minimum Payment	Excess (New Savings)	Monthly Payment
1) Credit Card	paid off	paid off	paid off	paid off
2) Credit Card	$5,156	$123.00	$1,570.00	$1,693.00
3) Credit Card	$8,011.00	$115.00	$0.00	$115.00
4) Credit Card	$14,289.00	$227.00	$0.00	$227.00
Totals	$27,456.00	$465.00	$1,570.00	$2,035.00

 Note: Credit cards #3 & #4 balances reflect two months of minimum payments made.

I calculated that in less than four months I would pay off credit card #2: ($5,156 balance/ $1,693 monthly payments = 3.045 months). $1693 x 4 months = $6772. This is how much four months worth of credit card #2 payments equaled. $6,772 - $5,156 (payment balance) = $ 1616. This is how much money I have left over in the fourth month after paying off credit card # 2. What do you think I did with that excess money? If you said, went on a wild shopping spree, maybe you need to read this book again. I applied the excess $1,616 toward my credit card #3, of course! By then, I had paid six months of minimum payments (2 months from the previous grid and 4 months now) to credit card # 3.That is a total of $690 [$115 (cc #3 min) x 6 months]. Add the $690 to the $1,616 excess money from credit card #2 pay off and I had lowered my credit card #3 balance by $2,306 to $5935 in only six months. In addition to lowering that balance, I also paid off TWO credit cards in the process. Hello!

Credit Card #3 new balance breakdown

Original credit Card #3 balance	$8,241
Six months of minimum payments	-$690
Money left over from paying off credit card #2	-$1,616
Total balance left on credit card #3	**=$5,935**

Once again, I created a new grid to reflect the fact that I now only had two credit cards, that now had lower balances. I also took $1,693, the excess monthly amount I *was* paying credit card #2 and added it to credit card #3's current minimum of $115. I applied all of it to credit card #3's new lowered balance ($5,935). I was now making a total payment of $1,808 to credit card #3 every month ($1,693 + $115 = $1,808).

	Balance	Monthly Minimum Payment	Excess (New Savings)	Monthly Payment
1) Credit Card	paid off	paid off	paid off	paid off
2) Credit Card	paid off	paid off	paid off	paid off
3) Credit Card	$5,935.00	$115.00	$1,693.00	$1,808.00
4) Credit Card	$13,381.00	$227.00	$0.00	$227.00
Totals	$19,316.00	$342.00	$1,693.00	$2,035.00

 Note: Credit card #4's balance reflects six months of minimum payments made.

Four must be my lucky number because I calculated that it would take another four months for me to pay off credit card # 3 ($5,935, card #3's balance / $1808, new monthly payments = 3.28), rounded up to four months. After completely paying off credit card #3, at the end of those four months, I had an excess of $1,297. That is ($5,935, card #3's balance) – ($1,808 x 4 months). I was getting used to the whole being responsible with my money thing again and I applied the $1,297 towards my last and final credit card. Whoo hooo! By that time, I had also reduced credit card #4 by 10 months worth of minimum payments ($227 x 10 months) $2,270. So my new balance for credit card #4 was $14,743 – ($2,270 + $1,297 excess from card #3 pay off) = $11,176.

Credit Card #4 new balance breakdown

Original credit Card #3 balance	$14,743
10 months of minimum payments	-$2,270 ($227 x 10 months)
Money left over from paying off credit card #3	-$1,297
Total balance left on credit card #4	=$11,176

I created my final grid to reflect my almost new-found freedom from credit cards! Three cards down and one last one to go! I applied $1808, the monthly payment of credit card # 3 and combined it with credit card #4's minimum $227 ($1,808 + $227 = $2,035) and paid off the last credit card in less than six months ($ 11,176 / $2,035 = 5.49 months).

	Balance	Monthly Minimum Payment	Excess (New Savings)	Monthly Payment
1) Credit Card	paid off	paid off	paid off	paid off
2) Credit Card	paid off	paid off	paid off	paid off
3) Credit Card	paid off	paid off	paid off	paid off
4) Credit Card	$11,176.00	$227.00	$1,808.00	$2,035.00
Totals	$11,176.00	$227.00	$1,808.00	$2,035.00

 Note: Notice that the total monthly credit card payments stayed the same on each payoff grid, $2,035. Your payoff grid should do the same. Do this by paying down one debt, then using all of that money to pay down the next debt. Don't spend it arbitrarily, willy nilly orfoolishly.

Imagine paying off a little over $31,000 of debt in about a year and four months! How did I get a year and four months you ask? The first credit card took about 2 months to pay off; the second and third cards took about 4 months and the last card around six months (2 + 4 +4 +6 =16 months). The key is, once you pay off one card, use all the monthly money you used to pay previous cards and apply it toward the next card on your list (including its monthly minimum). Doing this creates a snowball effect. So by the time you get to the last and highest balanced card, you are throwing some serious cash at it. Get it? A snowball rolling down the hill, gets bigger as it rolls. Got it? Just think if I hadn't been frozen with inaction for a year I could have wiped out my debt much faster. Are you frozen with fear and anxiety? Snap out of it and create your grids today!

The Budgetnista's Unexpected Money System:
I know that some of you may feel as though the system I described will take a long time to manifest. In layman's terms, you want to get rid of your debt sooner, not later. One of the ways I'm able to pay down my other debt even faster is by using my own system in conjunction with listing my debt and paying them down one by one. *The Budgetnista's Unexpected Money System* works like this: every single one of us, without fail, receives Unexpected Money in our lifetime. It can happen weekly, monthly or even yearly. I can already sense that some of you are shaking your heads and saying, "not me!" Bear with me and I will explain further.

"Unexpected Money" (UM) is *any* money received outside of your primary source of income, a.k.a. your J-O-B. Examples of "Unexpected Money" are: a raise, loan repayment (to you), refund (from taxes or returning of unwanted items), rebates (do you fill out and mail in those forms? I do!), found money, gifted money (happy birthday!). If you purchase an item that is on sale but don't realize it until you get to the cashier, the money you save is "Unexpected Money". You already planned to spend the money on the item, so you won't miss it if you use it for your debt reduction instead. If you have generous friends who occasionally surprise and treat you by paying for your meal, the money you were *going* to pay is also Unexpected Money. Cha-ching! Are you starting to see the possibilities here?

In a nutshell, "Unexpected Money" or UM, is any money that you did not expect to receive or save. It's money that does not normally contribute to your day-to-day living expenses. So, it's therefore not calculated into the new budget you now have. You *do* have a new budget, right?

Unfortunately, most UM is wasted, forgotten or magically disappears hours after it's received. Does that sound like you? In the Budgenista's world, UM is literally a Godsend for paying down debt, if used within 24 hours. By using UM in this way, you will expedite your Ultimate Debt-Free Day in ways that you cannot imagine. Here is an example of how I use UM. My youngest sister finally pays me back the $10 she owes me from months ago. Moments after receiving this unexpected bounty, I race to my computer and set up an automatic $10 payment from my Bills account to which ever credit card is currently receiving the lion's share of my excess money. I then transfer $10 dollars from my Deposit Account (where my cash allowance is waiting) to my Bills Account. I now know when the time comes to take out my weekly allowance (remember, I break down my bi-weekly allowance and pay myself each week), I will take out $10 *less* because I currently have $10 cash in hand. You may not always receive Unexpected Money in the form of petty cash. If you receive UM as a check or a larger lump sum of cash, simply deposit it directly into your Bills Account and set up an automated payment to your debt, for the amount you just deposited. I do this *every time* I am blessed to receive UM. Once in a period of two months I received over $4000 in Unexpected Money.

My Two Month $4,000 UM Breakdown

$1,500	Furniture Payments (I sold my furniture when I moved back home)
$400	Credit Card Point Redemption (you too may have reward points that are worth cash. Ask and see.)
$10	Little Sister Loan Repayment
$100	New Phone Rebate
$300	Garage Sale Proceeds (the money I made selling my things before I moved back home)
$300	Budget Jobs (money I received helping clients create their personal budgets)
$600	Tax Refund (my accountant found money I overpaid the government from two years ago. I love my accountant!)
$800	Insurance check (during the finalizing of this book, my car (yes the original), was totaled while parked. The responsible party paid dearly. This is what was left over after I got another used car)

$4,010	**Unexpected Money!!**

Believe me, when you start documenting your own "Unexpected Money" occurrences, you will not believe how much of it you actually receive. My two-month $4,010 example is not typical for me. But I do find myself receiving UM each month no matter how small. Don't worry, you'll find "Unexpected Money", even if it's just money left over from your cash allowance. That's UM too! The rule of thumb is any UM over $5 is put toward debt pay down. When debt is no longer an issue, it can be put toward savings, retirement or investing. After I pay down *all* of my debt (sans the mortgage), I plan to have a UM drawer where I would throw all of my UM for the month. At the end of each month, I will use my UM to add to my investments via my financial advisor or on my own through sites like sharebuilder.com and etrade.com.

"Unexpected Money" literally changed my life. It put me back in control and helped me to pay off my "Financial Fiasco" faster than I ever imagined. If you use it in conjunction with the **One Week Budget** and the "Get-Out-of-Debt-Snowball Plan", UM will change your life too.

Bonus Chapter
Debt and Credit Action Steps (Recap)

Here's a quick run-down of things to keep in mind when trying to reduce your debt and improve your credit rating. Following these steps is a sure-fire way to get your debts under control.

1) List all of your debt from lowest to highest.

2) Figure out how much money you can squeeze from your budget for your debt-pay-down plan (*New Savings*, Step 6). You don't have to use all of your *New Savings* like I did.

3) Pay only the minimum amount required on all your debt, with the exception of the one card you are trying to pay off. This should be the card or debt with the lowest amount owed.

4) Pay the minimum and the money you squeezed from your budget (the amount of *New Savings* you have dedicated to debt reduction) toward the first debt on your list.

5) Automate the payments. This will leave you with less work and tallying to do each month. Make sure you automate the payments to reflect how many months it will take to pay down whatever main debt you are focused on paying off. Then reset your automation when you move on to the next debt.

6) Use UM (Unexpected Money) to help pay down the main debt you're focused on.

7) After paying off the first credit card, apply ALL the money you used each month to pay off that card and put it towards the next card on your list. This means that the minimum amount from the first card, the minimum from the second and the extra money that you found in your budget (*New Saving*, Step 6) will be applied toward the next card on the list.

8) Automate this new payment. Remember: doing this will help you stick to your strategy.

9) Use UM to pay down this card.

10) Pay off the second card. Then, transfer all the money you were paying each month to that card and apply it towards the third card, along with its minimum.

I suggest you continue this cycle until you pay off *all* of your credit card debt! Once you are credit card debt free, use this system to pay off the rest of your debt and finance your savings, retirement and investment goals. Don't forget to keep a record of all Unexpected Money received and paid out on your Budget Grid.

thebudgetnista.biz

APPENDIX

Tips for Realistically Reducing Your Spending

Extra Blank Budget Grid Templates

Appendix
Tips for Realistically Reducing Your Spending
STEP 5

FIXED CHANGES
- Call your cable company. Tell them your bill is too high. Ask what they can do to help reduce it. No cable package is concrete. Channels can be shaved off to save you money. Many times, representatives may also have access to coupons that they can apply to your account.
- Before your lease expires, start looking for a less expensive apartment. You can pay as much as $200 less in rent a month by doing a little research.
- Shop around for car insurance, ask for multiple quotes. You can save hundreds of dollars each year by switching to a new, cost-effective company. Make sure, however, that the type of insurance you obtain will effectively cover all essentials should something happen.
- Raise the deductible on your car insurance. This can save you up to 30% a year.
- Auto-pay your bills through your bank. Some companies offer lower rates if you pay this way. My car insurance company does.
- Get a car alarm. Many insurance companies will drop your rate by as much as 15% if you have one.
- Depending on the age and value of your car, you may want to drop collision and comprehension coverage from your car insurance. This can save you upwards of 40% on your car insurance. Ask your insurance company representative for advice.
- If your car payments are too high, refinance with a different agency. Try your local credit union or look on www.bankrate.com for competitive rates.
- Consolidate student loans. This will enable you to lock in a low rate. It can also save you money with lower monthly payments. Only do so if the rate being offered is an advantageous one and the new loan timeline is reasonable.
- Use the Internet to shop around. Sites like www.bankrate.com can help you compare different financial institutions and the products they offer.

ADJUSTABLE CHANGES
- Save money on your gas bill by turning down the heat by 1-2 degrees.
- Save money on your electric bill by turning off unused lights and switching your current light bulbs to energy saving bulbs.
- Reduce appliance repair costs by registering them with your local energy supplier. For less than $15 a month, my local supplier will fix or replace my registered appliances. Be sure to read the fine print and ask questions, especially as it relates to replacing appliances.
- Instead of your credit card, use cash, or if you must, your debit card whenever possible.

- Pay off your credit card bill in full every month. Doing this will help you avoid costly finance charges.
- Save the money you need for big-ticket items and buy them with cash. Don't use your credit card! If you buy with cash, it will be easier to bargain for a lower price. The vendor will be able to avoid the credit card fee they pay when customers use credit cards, and will pass that savings on to you.
- Pay bills online or have them automatically taken from your account to avoid late fees.
- Drop overdraft protection at your bank. This will dramatically cut down on overdraft fees. If you don't have the funds, the transaction will just be denied (like the old days).
- Fill your car with regular gas. Using premium gas is an unnecessary expense, unless your car guide specifies its use.
- Call your credit card company and ask them to lower your rate. If you have good credit or have been a good customer for a number of years, your company should comply. Don't take no for an answer, let them know that you can always take your business elsewhere.
- Switch your high-interest credit card balances to a fixed lower interest card. Make sure the card's rate does not jump to a ridiculously high rate after the introductory period has passed. Remember to read the fine print and ask a lot of questions. Also, try asking your credit card company to extend the introductory rate. The worst they can say is no.
- If you routinely go over your cell phone plan minutes, increase your plan to save on overage fees. The monthly increase should be less than your average monthly overage fee.
- Cut prescription costs. Many employers use a Pharmacy Benefit Manager (PBM). Ordering your regular medication through your PBM can cut your co-payments by as much as 100%.
- Talk to your doctor about getting free samples of medicines for short term use, or until your regular medicines through your PBM arrive.
- If you have poor health insurance or none at all, use a teaching hospital. They often have clinics for dentistry, general health and a gynecological clinic. At the clinics in these hospitals, your payment is usually based upon your income.
- Don't be afraid to bargain. Remember persistence and politenesses are key to getting what you want.

EASILY ADJUSTABLE CHANGES
- When it comes to eating lunch at work, try bringing food from home. This will reduce eating out costs.
- Use coupons. You'll be surprised how much money you'll save.
- To help eliminate unnecessary grocery shopping, create a menu of meals each week.

thebudgetnista.biz

- Make a grocery list before going to the grocery store. On the list, include an estimated cost of items. Bring the amount you have estimated in cash. Be sure to leave your credit and debit card at home.
- Buy a filter or a filter water jug instead of bottled water.
- Do your research online before purchasing goods and services. You can always find books, electronics, furniture, music, etc. at discounted prices.
- Don't buy clothes or any other luxury items impulsively. Designate specific shopping days, estimate what you are willing to spend, and bring that amount with you in cash.
- Shop at thrift and consignment shops.
- Borrow books and videos from the library.
- Print out online coupons before shopping. Most of your favorite stores offer discounts this way.
- Rent movies instead of spending money at the theatre. Many grocery stores have a $1 a day movie rentals.
- Visit your local cobbler instead of buying new shoes. Spending just $10 to fix up your favorite shoes can save you hundreds in the long run.
- Be realistic when reducing spending. Continue to enjoy all the things your money provides, but in moderation.
- Remember, exercise *planned* spending and take what you need in cash.

BIG CHANGES

These are suggestions for those who are still spending more money than they make, even after realistically reducing their spending.

- Move back home with your parents. What?! *I did it for a short time.*
- Refinance your home.
- Modify your home loan.
- Defer your student loans.
- Get a roommate (s). *Did it!*
- Mow your own lawn.
- Insure your car(s) and home with the same company. By doing this, you may be eligible for a discounted rate. *Did this too!*
- Cut off your Internet unless it is absolutely necessary for your job or school. Use the library, it's FREE!
- If you have a home full of cell phones, consider dropping your landline. *I can't remember the last time I had a landline...*
- Get a cell phone family plan. Also, sign-up for a plan that offers unlimited service.
- Make sure you take advantage of the tax credits you qualify for by having children. Some of those include: American Opportunity Tax Credit, Annual Tuition Deduction, Child Tax Credit, and Dependent Care Credit. Ask your accountant about these programs.
- Trade in your car for a less expensive option. Affordable cars may not turn heads, but the extra cash spilling from your pockets will.

- Discontinue monthly recurring charges such as movies, subscriptions, gym (use the park), magazines, and clubs.
- Stop paying late fees by setting up automatic bill pay with your bank or just pay your bills online. This will help you to pay on time and avoid paying for postage. Sign up for free online banking.
- Here's a tip for college students. Rent your books from sites like chegg.com or campusbookrental.com.
- Get your college-bound child a 7 or 14 meal plan. You can always increase the number of meals if needed.
- Buy your child a Student Advantage discount card ($20). By doing this, he or she will save up to 15% on bus, train and air fare.
- Sign up for your company's flexible spending account. The accounts offer 35% or more off on expenses you pay for anyway.
- Sign up for customer rewards programs at all the places you regularly shop. There are many coupons that grocery stores only offer to reward card holders.
- Car pool.
- If feasible, ride your bike, or walk to work. *Seriously.*
- Does your job offer a transportation reimbursement account? Sign up today!
- Cut down on dry cleaning. If special care is taken, many items can be washed at home. Be sure to read the care directions before washing.
- Check to make sure that all your checking accounts are free.
- Cut off your cable service. It is a nonessential luxury for those who are living above their means. Besides, if you still have Internet access, you can watch movies and TV shows for free online at sites like hulu.com. It's all legal, of course. *I haven't had a T.V. in 4 years!*
- Do at home hair color touchups between hair coloring appointments.
- Get a second job. In order to maximize your time and money, your second job should be in a field related to what you already do for a living. For example, a teacher may want to work for an after school program or tutor. A janitor should seek additional employment as a handyman or part-time property manager. Working in a related field means you will not have to acquire another skill set and your compensation will most likely be greater due to your experience. Work overtime. Find a higher paying job. Use sites like craigslist.com, simplyhired.com, idealist.com, and indeed.com to job search. *I always do this!*
- Enlist the help of an employment agency to find another job.
- When looking for jobs, be specific about your salary needs. If you are unsure, check your budget and use sites like paycheckscity.com to calculate what your actual take-home pay will be, based upon your gross pay. By doing this, you will be able to know instantly how much money you will need to make a year in order to reach your monthly financial goals.

- If you own a house or condo, consider renting it out and moving into an apartment. You may be able to save over $1,000 a month as long as your rent covers most or your entire mortgage. Revamp your money list (Step 7) as if you moved out, to make sure that the cost of your apartment with utilities will still enable you to save a significant amount of money. *You already know I did this.*
- Consider using public transportation. Make sure that the cost is less than your monthly toll and gas consumption.
- Reduce the amount of times you go out. Choose free activities like game or movie nights at a friend's house.
- Do your own grooming: nails, hair, haircuts, eyebrows, etc. *I do this, but I'm not sure how well...*
- Barter your skills with a friend. Baby sitting for lawn mowing, etc.
- Suspend vacations.
- Cook inexpensive meals. Chicken, rice and beans are healthy yet frugal foods.

Finally, if you spend more money than you make and you cannot afford to live day to day, it's time to make big changes in your life. Stop spending money on all those nonessential items and organize your finances. I know there is some work involved when you initially set up the One Week Budget. But the only two steps you have to do ever again are Steps 7 and 12. Revamp Your Money List and Work the System.

For more FREE $ tips be sure to visit my blog!
I give great financial tips there! WWW.THEBUDGETNISTA.BIZ

Extra blank budget grid templates:

BUDGET GRID 1

MONTH you're paid:					
TOTAL TAKE HOME PAY	$				
TAKE HOME PAY(2) AMT.	$				
SOURCE					
DATE:					

ACCOUNT	DUE DATE	NAME & CONFIRMATION #	ESTIMATED AMOUNT	AMOUNT PAID	DATE PAID
			$	$	
			$	$	
			$	$	
			$	$	
			$	$	
			$	$	
			$	$	
			$	$	
			$	$	
			$	$	
			$	$	
			$	$	
BILL TOTAL			$	$	
TOTAL			$	$	

BUDGET GRID 2

MONTH you're paid:					
TOTAL TAKE HOME PAY	$				
TAKE HOME PAY(2) AMT.	$				
SOURCE					
DATE:					
ACCOUNT	DUE DATE	NAME& CONFIRMATION #	ESTIMATED AMOUNT	AMOUNT PAID	DATE PAID
			$	$	
			$	$	
			$	$	
			$	$	
			$	$	
			$	$	
			$	$	
			$	$	
			$	$	
			$	$	
			$	$	
			$	$	
BILL TOTAL			$	$	
TOTAL			$	$	

To My Reader,

It is my hope that you have taken away something of great value from this book. I hope that the hopeless feeling you've had about your finances has been eased. I hope that you feel empowered knowing that if I can dig my way out of my "Financial Fiasco", you can too! I hope that I've kept my promise to God by sharing the knowledge that I was blessed with in a way that was easy to understand and implement. Please don't forget to help others. Keep in mind that gifts are never yours alone to keep. I leave you with these parting words: Is a week's worth of work, worth a lifetime of financial empowerment? I hope you answered yes. Your blessings begin the moment you *allow* them to.

God Bless,

Tiffany Odochi Aliche (The Budgetnista)

Acknowledgments

First and foremost, I would like to give my most grateful thanks to God. He always blesses us. It is we who choose whether or not to allow our blessings to manifest.

I also want to thank Mommy, Daddy, and my sisters: Karen, Tracy, Carol and Lisa. You are my cheerleaders, my best friends, my sounding board, and my inspiration. Anyone who knows the *Aliche Girls*, knows how supportive we are of each other. Thank you.

To all my family both here and abroad, thank you for your constant love and support. The strong foundation you've provided is the reason I've been able to reach such heights.

Dreena Whitfield (WhitPR) and Sonya Ellis (Writeontime) thank you so much for helping me transform and polish my words into a book I can be proud of.

Mike, thanks for pushing me and then letting me fly.

Thank you MEDINA, Rafael & Sean, of MEDINA = CITI Design Firm. I came to you at crunch time and you more than delivered.

THND: We worked together, traveled together and grew together. I am eternally grateful for all that I've learned from each of you. Diesa E. Seidel, Joy Jackson and Nina Pilar.

Special thanks to Linda Iferika, Regina Garlin of RCG Mortgage, Herb Caesar, Toi Powell for creating my Budgetnista coin logo, Jackie Nwobu for leading the way and inspiring me, all my family, friends, coworkers, and all of my well wishers.

I especially want to thank those people who allowed me to help them create their personalized budget. You gave me more than I ever gave you. You are forever memorialized as the anecdotes in this book.

Tiffany 'The Budgetnista' Aliche, a New Jersey native earned her Bachelor's Degree in Business Administration from Montclair State University, she forwent a career in corporate America to teach underserved youth in Newark, NJ. She went on to continue her graduate studies at Seton Hall University in New Jersey.

Tiffany is a passionate teacher of financial empowerment. She has her own financial consulting company called CLD Financial Life LLC. CLD was created around the belief that the purpose of life is to live a life of service. Tiffany centers her service on helping others master their money. She began her journey to help empower communities through financial literacy by helping family and friends first and then extending her services to churches, schools, companies and various organizations. CLD Financial Life is the manifestation of her altruistic efforts to help others empower themselves financially.

In keeping with the mission of CLD, Tiffany wrote The One Week Budget. She can be reached via email at thebudgetnista@gmail.com and her blog, thebudgetnista.biz.

Find Tiffany:

Facebook:	facebook.com/thebudgetnista
Twitter:	@thebudgetnista
Youtube:	youtube.com/thebudgetnista
Blog:	thebudgetnista.biz